Mustard Seeds and Viral Videos

Mustard Seeds and Viral Videos

Modern Retellings of the Parables of Jesus

MATTHEW EDWARDS

Foreword by Leonard Sweet

RESOURCE *Publications* · Eugene, Oregon

MUSTARD SEEDS AND VIRAL VIDEOS
Modern Retellings of the Parables of Jesus

Resource Publications
An Imprint of Wipf and Stock Publishers
199 W. 8th Ave., Suite 3
Eugene, OR 97401

www.wipfandstock.com

PAPERBACK ISBN: 978-1-6667-4941-0
HARDCOVER ISBN: 978-1-6667-4942-7
EBOOK ISBN: 978-1-6667-4943-4

VERSION NUMBER 030623

To Brooke

Contents

Foreword

"There is no now." With these words, Italian theoretical physicist Carlo Rovelli, called "the new Stephen Hawking," presents what he calls "the most astounding conclusion arrived at in the whole of contemporary physics."[1] There is no "present." The "now" does not exist except as a localized illusory, soapy bubble. There is only a past and a future.

We live in the overlap between the past and the future. Catch me a present. Did you pull it in? Can you carpe diem and lock it in place? The present is gone faster than the snap of a finger. In a strict sense, there is no carpe diem, only carpe manana or carpe pasada. Heaven is The Eternal NOW . . . The everlasting present. Our use of the term "present" is a metaphor for the already/not-yet, that overlap between future becoming past. In the words of Dr. Edwards, "In this overlap of the ages, the 'already but not yet,' the kingdom of God is at hand . . . but also something to be looked forward to."

We live out of the past, not in it. Like the flow of a swing, we lean back to remake the past anew, not just to curate the tradition but to kick forward and redeem and renew the tradition. Tradition is a verb, an activity that does more than conserve the past but to conceive the new from congress with the old.[2]

This is what Matthew Edwards has done with the parables of Jesus. With a sacred imagination that is as stunning as it is sparkling, he has taken ten of them, and prepared for us some fresh bread by baking them in the context of the culture that is forming around us. At the end of each chapter discussion questions encourage and facilitate small group study.

1. Rovelli, *The Order of Time.*
2. Lerer, *Tradition: A Feeling for the Literary Past.*

Paradoxically, living out of the ancientfuture "overlap" primes us to be in a state of "allthereness" in every moment, fully present to the presence of the "kingdom come" so that you know your best moments in life: when you're eating your best steak, or preaching your best sermon, or seeing your best sunset.

Carlo Rovelli was not the first to identify the flow and flex of time. Søren Kierkegaard called the present a place marker between the past and the future and, as such, it didn't really exist in any meaningful way. He was arguing hard against Hegel and the various influencers of his age who wanted to "live in the present" and "forget the past." Kierkegaard's answer? You can't live in something that doesn't really exist, except in the conception of God and eternity. Tradition is not something that ties us to the past but launches us into the future. This book traditions us for the future.

Biblical scholar N. T. Wright, in *Surprised by Scripture* (2015), makes the helpful distinction between building the kingdom of God, which is not biblical, and the biblical notion of building *for* the kingdom of God, where all we do that is of value in all arenas of life is taken up into God's comprehensive renewal of the cosmos. Do goodness, beauty, and truth, and God does the rest. When you read *Mustard Seeds and Viral Videos: Modern Retellings of the Parables of Jesus*, you are scaffolding the soul and traditioning your life for God's construction of a new creation and ageless future.

Leonard Sweet
Drew University
George Fox University
Northwind Seminary

Preface

THIS BOOK WAS TWELVE years in the making. In 2009, my colleague Gary Albert suggested we preach a sermon series on the parables of Jesus. As I researched and outlined my sermons for the series, I realized I was not going to do them justice. The parables pack an emotional punch. They shock us. They bring us to tears. They make us angry. When Jesus told the parable of the tenants, the Pharisees responded by plotting to kill him.

Were my sermons going to have the same impact as Jesus's stories? Clearly not.

This got me thinking about how so much preaching robs the Scriptures of their artistic power. Sermons on the parables are perhaps the worst offenders. I decided in that moment to try something different: instead of preaching on the parables, I was going to *retell* the parables in modern settings. I spent the summer of 2009 writing and then preaching six of the stories included in this book.

The results were polarizing. I heard feedback to the tune of "You can't do this in church" and "We want a sermon, not 'story time with Matt.'" At the same time, people came up to me in tears telling me that the parables spoke to them in powerful new ways through my stories. An unchurched foreign exchange student brought one Sunday by his host family told me, "If they did things like this in church in Germany, I think I would go." My mind went back to the emotional response that Jesus's own stories had on people, and I realized I must have done something right.

In 2021, my church came back to the parables. By then I had a doctorate in ministry and teenagers instead of toddlers. I wrote four more stories, updated some of the 2009 ones, and put the finishing touches on what became this book. My hope is that by reading it, you have a fresh encounter with some of Jesus's most inspiring portrayals of the kingdom of God.

This book would not have happened without help from many people. Thank you to Gary Albert and the people of Believers Fellowship for trusting me to take a creative approach to preaching the parables. It brings great joy to my soul to serve in an environment where I can take artistic risk when telling the story of God. Thank you to Leonard Sweet and my SFS12 DMin cohort at Portland Seminary for stretching me in my approach to preaching and storytelling. Wrestling with semiotics alongside such gracious, Spirit-filled, and intelligent men and women changed my life. You are truly kingdom pioneers! Thank you to my readers: Caitlin Honig, Heather Cummings, and Lisa Anderson, and my editor Rochelle Deans. Feedback can be hard to hear, but your suggestions were invaluable to improving the quality of this work. Thank you for caring enough to tell me what could be better! Thank you to my kids: Zack, Avery, and Luke. Even writing your names brings a smile to my face. Thank you for putting up with my anxiety and self-doubt and for always thinking the best of me.

Finally, thank you to my wife, Brooke. In many ways this book is a joint effort as I would have quit long ago without your support. Thank you for being in my corner. Often, your love, compassion, and encouragement are the only things that keep me going. I have never met anyone else as beautiful, smart, caring, and devoted as you, and I am so happy that we are journeying this thing called life together. I love you.

Introduction

WHEN THE BALLERINA ISADORA Duncan was once asked backstage what a particular dance meant, she responded, "If I could explain it with words, I wouldn't have to dance."

Sometimes, the medium *is* the message.

Jesus used parables to preach the kingdom of God. Think about the difference in these two statements from Jesus. First, "Why do you call me 'Lord, Lord,' and not do what I tell you?"[1] Second:

> Everyone who comes to me and hears my words and does them, I will show you what he is like: he is like a man building a house, who dug deep and laid the foundation on the rock. And when a flood arose, the stream broke against that house and could not shake it, because it had been well built. But the one who hears and does not do them is like a man who built a house on the ground without a foundation. When the stream broke against it, immediately it fell, and the ruin of that house was great.[2]

Both statements make the same point: It is not enough just to acknowledge the truth of Jesus's words; we must also obey them.

The first statement gets right to the point. It is propositional and economic. There is no disputing or misunderstanding the message. The second statement is a story. It is more artistic and engaging. I can imagine the man building his house on the sand and I catch myself thinking "What a fool!" But in thinking that, I condemn *myself* because I hear Jesus without obeying. The artistry of the story makes me want to be like the wise builder who builds on the rock. The message is more difficult to discern, but it hits me in

---

1. Luke 6:46.
2. Luke 6:47–49.

the heart in a way a straight proposition cannot. It makes me *want* to obey. It makes me *desire* the kingdom of God.[3]

This is where the parables of Jesus come in. Through his stories, Jesus taught us how to see the kingdom of God. It is not enough for us to understand the kingdom of God, we must also desire it.

Think about the art on the walls of fitness centers. Are the walls covered in information—diagrams of stretches, exercises, or routines? No—they are covered with images of people in peak physical fitness. Mid-workout, when you don't know if you can get that extra repetition in or whether you can get that extra mile on the treadmill, you look at the wall and you see an image of the kind of body you might have someday if you stay the course. Your imagination is stirred, and you are motivated to persevere.

The kingdom of God is any place where God is reigning. While God is the true king of the universe, the Scriptures teach us that creation has rebelled against its king. The Scriptures tell us that this rebellion, called sin, is the cause of strife, violence, poverty, disease, and death. But the Scriptures teach that Jesus Christ *defeated* sin and death through the cross and his resurrection. One day, he will return and reconcile all creation to the rule of God. But in the meantime, God has sent the Holy Spirit into the world where he is at work building his kingdom through the proclamation of the gospel and the work of the saints.

We live in an overlap of ages. The old age of sin was defeated, and the new age of righteousness and peace has dawned. But the old is not yet completely gone and the new is not yet completely here. We live in a tension.

If you've ever resigned at a job and had to train your replacement, you are familiar with the concept of an overlap of the ages. When you resign, it represents the end of an era. Your time with the company is coming to an end, and a date is put on the calendar when the old will be done. But until that date, you continue in your role. If you train your replacement, there is a sense that "the new guy" is the new reality. Until you fulfill your obligations, there is overlap of the ages.

In this overlap of the ages, the "already but not yet," the kingdom of God is at hand! That said, the kingdom of God is *also* something to be looked forward to. Right now, we experience the kingdom of God in part in a real way. When Jesus returns, we will experience the kingdom of God in its fullness.

---

3. I am borrowing a phrase from James K.A. Smith.

I see the kingdom of God when my church works for justice and shalom. I see it when I pray over struggling husbands and wives and they receive the healing words of the gospel. I see it when my son plays piano. I see it when my daughter introduces herself to a new girl at church and welcomes her to the group. I see it when my wife comes alongside struggling homeschool moms and encourages them by assuring them that they *can* do it.

We catch glimpses of the kingdom of God every day if we train our eyes to see them.

This brings us back to Isadora Duncan's statement: "If I could explain it with words, I wouldn't have to dance." Duncan used dance to express things that she couldn't with any other sign. I did my doctoral work in semiotics (a ten-dollar word for "the study of signs"). People use all kinds of signs to communicate ideas—they use words, they use art, they use ballet, they use music, and more. Jesus used *parables* to describe the kingdom of God. Like Duncan and her dances, if Jesus could have described the kingdom with *propositions*, he wouldn't have had to tell stories. He told stories because that was the best way to get us to desire the kingdom.

The advantage of teaching in parables is that they speak to our hearts in ways propositions cannot. The disadvantage is that the meaning of the story isn't always obvious. What does it mean that the kingdom of God is like a widow who went to an unjust judge for justice? What does it mean that the kingdom of God is like a sower who went out to sow? Further complicating matters is that Jesus' stories are 2,000 years old, and the world has changed a lot since then. Jesus uses now-defunct religious orders, ancient agricultural techniques, antiquated dining etiquette, and foreign customs to illustrate his points. Many times, a straightforward reading without background knowledge leaves you scratching your head wondering what the story means.

Often, preachers like me solve this problem by preaching the parables in propositional terms. We think that if we can clarify the *meaning* of the parable so that people understand the *point*, that we can get people to desire the kingdom. But just like how explaining the punchline of a joke makes it no longer funny, explaining the meaning of a parable robs it of its emotional power.

That's where this book originated.

The following ten chapters contain ten stories about the kingdom of God. Instead of explaining a parable of Jesus in propositions, I have attempted to explain them while maintaining the original medium: a story. Each story is a modern retelling of one of Jesus's parables. Think of them as really long fictional sermon illustrations. They aren't translations of the parables. They aren't the word of God. They are stories. I think they might help you better understand the teaching of Jesus with all its punch.

Keep in mind that the stories are *fictional*. None of them are based on real events. The thoughts, feelings, and attitudes of the characters don't necessarily represent my own. In fact, some of them are intentionally offensive. (You realize some of Jesus's parables offended people, right?)

After each story, I have included the text of the original parable as Jesus told it. Then, I have a brief discussion where I *do* explain the parable in propositions and connect it to the story I wrote. Finally, I have discussion questions at the end of each chapter so that you can use the book in a small group study.

One of my favorite quotes is attributed to Antoine de Saint-Exupery: "If you want to build a ship, don't drum up people together to collect wood and don't assign them tasks and work, but rather teach them to long for the endless immensity of the sea."

That's my hope for this book. I hope that as you make your way through these parables that you begin to "long for the immensity of the sea." I hope these stories make you desire the kingdom of God. I hope you learn to see the work of God all around you. I hope you *feel* the kingdom. After all, if I could get you to *feel* the kingdom with propositions, I wouldn't have to tell stories.

Sweet Sixteen

"No longer do I call you servants, . . . but I have called you friends." (John 15:15)

You think you know a person. You think, after working with someone for ten years, that you've got them all figured out, but then you realize that everything you thought you knew was wrong. That's what happened to me. I was wrong about Tom Maguire. Just when I thought I had him all figured out, he did something so off the wall that I realized I knew nothing.

Tom owned one of the most successful commercial real estate development companies in the L.A. area, and I guess his family got left behind on his trip to the top. His wife, Cathy, left him ten years ago for her personal trainer and took their six-year-old daughter, Amber, with her. Tom felt terrible about the divorce, but the thing he regretted most was the toll it took on Amber. He hated that his little girl had to suffer the consequences of all the "adult stuff" he and Cathy went through.

With Cathy out of his life, Tom needed help. You wouldn't exactly call him the most organized person on earth. Without Cathy's help, he double-booked appointments, missed crucial meetings, and drowned in his inbox. I guess Cathy just took care of all of that stuff for him. It's funny how someone so brilliant in one sphere could be so incompetent in another. Tom could mesmerize clients with his understanding of market trends and cost-benefit analysis. But ask him who his dentist is, and you just get a blank stare.

Tom was desperate for a personal assistant right around the time I graduated from UCLA, and I was offered the position. My parents were against it at first. "Holly," they asked me, "Why is this forty-year-old man hiring a 22-year-old woman to be his personal assistant? Something's not right here." Besides, I wasn't really the personal assistant type. I had an academic scholarship and graduated second in my class. I was more of the get-an-MBA-and-work-for-a-Fortune-500-company type. But Tom's charisma won me over and I took the job. Fortunately, my parents were wrong about Tom. He was married to his company and his interest in me was strictly professional.

After working with Tom for ten years, I thought I had him figured out. I knew what style of shirt he liked, what he didn't like, and how to convince him to like the ones that actually looked good. I knew which appointments he'd miss if I didn't remind him. I knew his mother's birthday, even though he always forgot. We went through a lot in that decade. I saw him close multi-million dollar deals with ease, and I watched him grieve the loss of his father. We saw good times and hard times, but the hardest time for *me* was when his daughter Amber decided to move back in.

Cathy's relationship with the personal trainer was short-lived, and afterward she bounced from one guy to another. When Amber was twelve, she had had enough and asked if she could move in with dad. Tom may have been a workaholic, but at least Amber didn't have to compete with any flavors-of-the-month for his affection.

When Amber moved in, Tom changed. She had him wrapped around her finger. Whatever she wanted—from a bichon fries to a designer hand-bag—she got. Further, Amber *hated* me. She talked down to me, rolled her eyes at everything I said, and went out of her way to make my life painful. And Tom wasn't much help with the whole situation. Whenever I tried to talk to him about Amber's behavior, he laughed it off and found some way to take her side.

I think Amber hated me because she saw me as a replacement for her mom. Even though my relationship with Tom was strictly professional, I can see how Amber saw things differently. After all, I had to do a lot of the "mom" things. I picked her up at school. I made her dinner. And when she "needed" this season's must-have accessory, I was the one who took her shopping to get it.

Now, to be fair, I gave Amber as much attitude as she gave me. But she was a brat. She had no idea how good she had it—what opportunities were open to her, and where she could go in life if she just applied herself.

I had none of those things growing up. I came from a working-class family, but my dad worked just as much as Tom. My parents spent every dime they made trying to give me and my brothers an opportunity. The beauty of America, they told me, was that *anyone* could succeed if they worked hard enough. And they certainly modeled that for me.

When I was seven years old, we moved to one of nicer neighborhoods in L.A., even though we probably shouldn't have afforded it. We went there for the schools. My dad put in overtime every week to cover the mortgage and make sure that we were in the best school system possible.

Amber reminded me of all the rich kids I grew up with. They skated through life because they knew that mommy and daddy were going to get them into college and pay for it. America may be the Land of Opportunity, but it is the Land of Bigger Opportunity if you have money.

So, given my relationship with Amber, you could understand my re-luctance to take on Tom's latest project. We were in his office one Monday morning going over the schedule for the week. I reminded him that we still needed to get back to the county about the Werderman project, and that

Amber had a dentist appointment on Wednesday. He detailed me on last week's meetings and some projects he had in the works. The meeting was just like every other Monday morning, until we finished and I was gathering my things.

"Oh, one more thing." Tom said. He said it like this "one more thing" had been on his mind all morning and he just didn't know how to tell me.

"Yes..." I responded cautiously.

"Amber's birthday is coming up..." he began.

"March 12," I interrupted. He probably needed me to pick up a present for her.

"Right. This is a big one. She's turning sixteen, you remember."

I did.

"I want to throw her a party. A huge one—something absolutely crazy. I want this to be the biggest bash she has ever seen—something like you'd see on one of those sweet sixteen reality shows."

I knew the shows. In fact, when he said that I thought about how funny it would be to see Amber on one of those shows. She was perfect for it—spoiled brat, dad can't say no, a nightmare for any poor person in charge of organizing the thing.

"I want you to organize the thing," Tom interrupted my daydreaming. I froze. Did he just say what I thought he said?

"Tom, I don't think I would be best for that. Amber and I have one of those relationships..."

"Nonsense," Tom cut in. "You're perfect. There is going to be a ton of details, and no one is as good at that stuff as you are. Besides, you know her, and you know what she likes."

I did know what she liked—expensive stuff. I also knew what she didn't like—me. He couldn't be serious. I could handle shopping for him. I could handle reminding him of things he should remember himself. I could even handle picking his daughter up from school. But not this. *This* was going too far.

"Seriously. I think you should find someone else."

"I don't want to find someone else. Holly, I want this to be special. Amber is my little girl. I don't want a stranger putting this together—and I would ruin it myself. I *need* your help. Please. I will forever be in your debt."

"You're already forever in my debt for saving you on the Douglas brothers' project last year," I reminded him.

"Oh yeah." He laughed. "Well, I'll be in an even bigger debt to you."

I could tell I wasn't going to get out of this. Tom wasn't where he was because he had poor negotiating skills. One way or another, I was going to end up planning that party. Maybe it wouldn't be so bad. Maybe I was wrong about Amber. Besides, it was just a party. How hard could it be?

***

Unfortunately, it didn't take long for me to realize *just* how hard it could be. Working with Amber was dreadful. She couldn't make up her mind about anything, and when she finally *did* decide, the next day she would change her mind. Two florists had already stopped returning my calls in frustration, and Bill from Gloria's Catering warned me never to bring Amber near their store again.

Three weeks before the party, Amber still hadn't found a dress. I must have taken her to every boutique in L.A. We decided to make a repeat visit to Fabiana's, bringing Tom along for moral support. Amber was trying on this horrid red strapless dress while I questioned her about decorations. Tom was outside chatting on his cell phone as the saleswoman fawned over how beautiful Amber looked in the awful red gown. Amber didn't look convinced.

"So, have you decided what you want to do with the cake table?" I asked Amber. "I have a couple ideas of how we can implement the swan theme."

As soon as these words came out of my mouth, Amber gave me "the look." "The look" says "Watch out. I hate you and I am about to make your life difficult." I braced myself as Amber stared in the mirror, searching for the words.

"This dress is hideous," she finally announced. "I think I'd rather wear a burlap sack. Do you have anything that actually looks good?"

I could see the frustration on the saleswoman's face. She had already had enough of Amber. She glared at me, as if asking, "Why did you bring this monster into my shop?" I shot back a look that said, "Welcome to my life."

"About the swan theme." Amber finally answered my question. "Kimberly thinks it would be cooler to do a Hollywood theme. You know, make the party feel like the Oscars. I think that would be epic."

I laughed nervously. Where did I start? We had swan-themed invitations ready to mail. I ordered special swan-shaped butter patties to be custom-made for every place setting. I had even arranged for a giant swan ice sculpture to be the focal point of the reception hall. Amber had to be kidding about this whole Hollywood nonsense. I chewed on my lip tensely as the saleswoman returned with more dresses for Amber to try on. They all looked ridiculous to me—like things a five-year-old would put on a Barbie. But Amber lit up when she saw them. Maybe I *was* getting old.

"You know, Amber, the party is only a few weeks away. I've made a lot of arrangements—the invitations are finished, and we ordered the ice sculpture. We can't change that stuff now. There's just not enough time."

Amber scowled at me. "Well, you're going to have to find a way because I hate the swan idea." She loved it yesterday. "The ice sculpture model looks like a chicken. I don't want chickens at my party." Seriously? Was she going there?

Amber put on a sparkly purple dress. I grimaced at the sight, but Amber was beaming. "It doesn't look like a chicken." I said to her. "And we already paid for all this stuff, and we can't get our money back."

"Who cares?" Amber shot back. "We can afford it. It's not like we're white trash or anything," she said, laughing. The saleswoman gave me another look. I glared back at her. "She's not *my* daughter," I told her with my eyes. If you have a problem with this little brat, take it up with her dad. He's right outside.

And that reminded me, Tom *was* just outside. I could get him to settle this dispute once for all. I went outside to get him.

"Would you mind coming in here. We need your input on something."

Tom hung up his phone and came into the dressing room.

"You saw the ice sculpture model. Did it look like a chicken?"

Tom laughed. "Yeah, it *did* kind of look like a chicken."

I rolled my eyes. "You're not helping," I said as I hit him with my planner. "The party is only a few weeks away and Amber wants to change things that we don't have time to change. We won't get our money back. Can you explain to her that we need to stick with what we decided?"

Amber gave Tom this look like a little girl who just lost her puppy. Tom shuffled his feet nervously, and then looked at me. "Holly, I want this party to be special for my little girl. If she doesn't like the ice chicken, we can change it to whatever she wants."

I almost dropped my planner.

"Thank you, Daddy!" Amber yelled as she threw her arms around him.

"Tom..." I started.

"Please. This is her big day. I want it to be perfect. Do whatever you can. You can make it happen."

Did he have any idea what he was saying? There was *no way* I could change the theme and put together a party on such short notice. NO way. I couldn't believe Tom. Why couldn't he stand up to his daughter? It was *his* fault she was so bratty. He had no backbone. She *knew* she had him wrapped around her finger, and she was going to milk it for everything she could for the rest of her life. They both infuriated me.

My parents taught me how to work hard. *My* parents taught me responsibility. *My* parents taught me that there are no free rides and that you have to earn things in life. Maybe Tom didn't realize it, but Amber's changes weren't just going to appear out of thin air. *I* was going to have to make them. *I* was going to have to work overtime. Once again, Tom let Amber make a mess that *I* had to clean up.

I glared at Amber. She was glowing as she hugged her dad. She relaxed a little and stuck her tongue out at me. What a monster.

***

Well, despite my insistence to the contrary, I *was* able to make all the changes Amber demanded. *All of them.* In fact, I put together such a brilliant party that I even amazed myself. We rented out this perfect old dive downtown and, after spending a fortune on decorations, it actually felt elegant.

On the day of the party, I was frantic. As always, *I* had to ensure that everything happened on cue. I had to coordinate caterers, waiters, bussers, and the MC. The decorators showed up an hour late, and they were in a frenzy trying to set everything up on time. Fifteen minutes before showtime, I was chewing out a sloppy florist when a waiter approached me sheepishly.

"What is it?" I demanded.

He braced himself as he spoke. "Uh, the birthday girl is crying in her dressing room. I was told that I should tell you."

What was she upset at now? Was the red carpet the wrong shade? I gave the florist one last order and then I headed back to Amber's dressing room.

I found her sobbing. "What is it?" I asked harshly.

Amber looked up at me. Her makeup was running and her face was flushed. "No one is coming!" she said through her tears.

"What do you mean no one is coming? We invited 300 people to this party."

"Look outside! No one is here!" she shouted, and then buried her face in her hands.

I left Amber in her room and made my way to the front door. I peered outside. Sure enough, no one was waiting to come in. I checked my watch—five minutes before the doors were supposed to open. I panicked. Why wasn't anyone here? What went wrong? Did the invitations go out? Was the wrong date on them? Was the map wrong? How could this happen? It was *Amber's* fault. She changed too much. If she just let me do things my way this would have been perfect. If only her dad had a backbone.

I ran back to Amber's dressing room. "What happened?"

"I don't know, but no one can come." I could barely understand her through the crying.

What was she talking about? How do you invite 300 people to a $100,000 party and have no one show up? How is that possible?

"Did you talk to your friends?" I asked.

"I did. They're not coming," she replied.

"What? How? What did they say?"

"Jessica said she didn't want to miss the season finale of *The Voice*. Preston and Connor are going to open mic night at Smitty's. And William is picking up extra shifts at work to save for a car."

"Seriously?" I asked. "Surely this is a joke. Do they know how big this party is going to be?"

"I told them," Amber sobbed. "But they can't come."

This was ridiculous. It was surreal. Surely I was dreaming. What teenager passes up on a party like this to watch a television show? But where are *Tom's* friends? I know he invited people to come celebrate with him. I called Tom's buddy Chuck. They had gone to college together and had stayed in touch over the years.

"Hello, Chuck?" I asked when he answered the phone. "This is Holly. Did you get the invitation to Amber's sweet sixteen party?"

"Oh yeah." Chuck said. "I wish I could make it. I have some things around the house that I have to do."

"Are you serious?"

"Yeah, I'm serious. Why would I joke about that? I really have to get these things done. My wife is starting to get mad."

I hung up on him. Was this whole city going nuts? Was there an epidemic of crazy going around? I would kill to go to a party like this and the guests were turning it down like it was an invitation to a time share informational meeting.

What was I going to do? I didn't know how it was possible, but *no one* was going to show up to this party. We had worked so hard and spent so much money. And Amber was a wreck. What would I tell Tom?

***

I found Tom sitting at the bar chatting gleefully with one of the waiters. I made my way over to him and rehearsed what I was going to say. I dreaded his reaction. I couldn't understand how this happened. I did *everything* right. How could this party have failed so miserably?

"Tom," I started. "We have a problem."

"Excuse me." Tom said to the waiter as he turned to me, smiling. "What is it, Holly? Everything looks great. The decorations are fantastic and the food smells delicious. It looks like a million bucks. It almost cost that much, too." He laughed.

"Yeah... it's not about any of that stuff. It's about the guests. They're not coming."

"Who's not coming?" Tom asked.

"No one is coming. There is no one here."

"No one?"

"No one."

"Wow. That *is* a problem. How is Amber taking it?"

"She's hysterical. This is a catastrophe. What are we going to do?"

"Well, we need to come up with some guests, quickly."

"Who are we going to call? We invited everyone we know."

"How about you?" he asked me.

"Me?" I didn't know what to say.

"You have the night off. You are not allowed to work tonight."

"But, Tom, what about the..."

"Holly, please. You have the night off. I want you to celebrate my daughter's sixteenth birthday with me—as a friend, not as an employee."

I was speechless.

"So, we have one guest. Who else can we invite?"

"Tom, there is nothing else around here. Ever since they built the rescue mission down the street, businesses have been hesitant to move in..."

"The rescue mission!" Tom exclaimed. "I bet there are some people there who have some free time!"

"Well, yeah. Of course they have free time. They're homeless."

"Let's bring 'em!"

Tom looked more excited than I had ever seen him. He really thought it was a good idea to invite homeless people to his daughter's sweet sixteen party.

"Okay," I said. "I'll head over there and get them."

"No," Tom said. "You have the night off. Remember? *I'll* go."

At that, he pulled out his cell phone and started dialing as he hurried toward the door.

"Hi. Is this KADO news? My name is Tom Maguire. I have a story for you."

At that he was gone—out the door and off to the rescue mission. This was crazy. There was no way this was going to work.

***

But you know what? It *did* work. Thirty minutes later, Tom returned with 200 homeless people in tow. You should have seen them when they entered the club. They were like kids entering Willy Wonka's Chocolate Factory—eyes wide open and mouths agape. Some made a beeline for the caterers. Others marveled at the flowers and ice sculpture. Some just stood there and tried to take everything in. It was like something out of a dream. None of them had ever been to an event like this. They didn't know what to do.

Soon enough, wonder turned into celebration. Amber came out of her dressing room to see what was going on and the room went nuts. They all shouted in unison, "Happy birthday!" and raised their glasses in the air. Some started clapping. Others were cheering. Amber's face lit up at the sight. Then, the music started playing and people started to dance. Amber danced with her dad as the guests surrounded them and cheered them on. I had never seen her look so happy.

I couldn't believe that Tom's plan worked. I thought he was crazy for going to the rescue mission, but the guests he brought sure knew how to party. I'm guessing they hadn't ever received an invitation like *this* before.

Shortly after Tom relocated the rescue mission to his daughter's party, a news crew arrived on the scene. One of the waiters motioned a reporter toward me. She asked me, "Did I hear right that Tom Maguire invited homeless people to this outlandish celebration? Has the host lost his mind?"

I laughed. "No. He hasn't lost his mind.... He just loves his daughter and wants to celebrate." It's funny what people will do for their kids.

I finished talking to the news crew and then went to find Tom. He was at the bar talking to a guy who had a scraggly beard running down past his chest. Next to him was a guy wearing a flannel shirt that looked like it hadn't been washed... ever. They were all drinking sparkling cider out of champagne flutes and laughing like lifelong friends. I wondered what they were thinking, partying like this.

Tom saw me coming and got up from his chair. "Great idea," he shouted as he walked toward me. "These people really know how to celebrate!" As he said that, the crowd around him shouted and lifted their glasses. They spontaneously erupted into a round of "Happy birthday to Amber." Tom laughed. Seeing people celebrate his daughter made him giddy. "Hey there's more room," he said. "We can invite more people. I'm going outside to see who is hanging out. Let's pack this place full. People are going to be talking about this party for years." Tom was glowing from ear to ear. He started heading toward the door when my cell phone rang.

"Hello?" I asked.

"Holly? This is Chuck. I saw your party on the news. It looks like a blast. You know, I think I might be able to come after all. How do I get there?"

"Hi Chuck," I started, but Tom grabbed the cell phone out of my hand and closed it. I looked at him, dumbfounded.

"That was your friend Chuck. He wants to come to the party."

"Why didn't he come earlier? Why did he have to see it on the news? If he was my friend, wouldn't he already be here?"

I didn't have an answer.

"If any of the other invited guests call; don't answer," he said. "My friends are all here." He had a point. "By the way, where *is* Amber?" He saw her and went across the room to wish her happy birthday.

I watched as Tom threw his arms around his daughter. She was wearing the ridiculous purple dress and the tears had been replaced by a magnificent smile. This really *was* the best party ever. I couldn't help but laugh at the whole scene. Who'd have thought? Amber really *does* have him wrapped around her finger. But... maybe that's not a bad thing. Maybe Tom isn't spineless. Maybe he is gracious. I mean, after all, who doesn't like to give good gifts to their children?

I started thinking about my own parents. Maybe they weren't so different from Tom. My dad worked overtime every week so that I could get a good education. That's how he loved his kids. Tom was doing the same thing, in his own way. I guess there is something about having kids that makes you crazy. Maybe someday I'll have kids and I'll understand.

Tom danced with his daughter as the poor, the downtrodden, and the outcast celebrated with them. It was the most beautiful sight I had ever seen. I felt bad for those who didn't respond to the call. They didn't know what they were missing. I lifted my glass. Happy birthday, Amber.

"When one of those who reclined at table with him heard these things, he said to him, 'Blessed is everyone who will eat bread in the kingdom of God!' But he said to him, 'A man once gave a great banquet and invited many. And at the time for the banquet he sent his servant to say to those who had been invited, "Come, for everything is now ready." But they all alike began to make excuses. The first said to him, "I have bought a field, and I must go out and see it. Please have me excused." And another said, "I have bought five yoke of oxen, and I go to examine them. Please have me excused." And another said, "I have married a wife, and therefore I cannot come." So the servant came and reported these things to his master. Then the master of the house became angry and said to his servant, "Go out quickly to the streets and lanes of the city, and bring in the poor and crippled and blind and lame." And the servant said, "Sir, what you commanded has been done, and still there is room." And the master said to the servant, "Go out to the highways and hedges and compel people to come in, that my house may be filled. For I tell you, none of those men who were invited shall taste my banquet."' (Luke 14:15–24)

In Luke chapter 7, some of John the Baptist's disciples come up to Jesus and ask him if he was the one to come or if there was going to be someone even greater. The question led into a discussion about Jesus and John and why the religious authorities of the day rejected them. John was an ascetic—the guy lived in the desert and ate bugs. Apparently, this freaked a lot of people out.

Jesus was different. Jesus says about the religious authorities' rejection of him and John: "John the Baptist has come eating no bread and drinking no wine, and you say, 'He has a demon.' The Son of Man has come eating and drinking, and you say, 'Look at him! A glutton and a drunkard, a friend of tax collectors and sinners!'"[1]

Think about that accusation for a second. Jesus was accused of being a drunkard. He was accused of being a glutton. Neither accusation was true, but they both had to have a *sliver* of truth to be believable.

1. Luke 7:33–34.

13

Jesus knew how to party, and he often partied with sketchy people.

The parable of the great banquet in Luke 14 might be my favorite portrayal of the kingdom of God. I love the thought of God going all out on a party (like a rich person throwing a sweet sixteen party for a beloved child). Outsiders might shake their heads and wag their fingers at God's lavish generosity, but He doesn't care.

The kingdom of God is a celebration, and *everyone* is invited. How many of our churches would be described like that?

A few years ago, I regained contact with an old friend from high school whom I hadn't talked to for many years. Our lives had taken very different paths since the glory days—me to seminary and him to adventure. He told me the tales of where he'd been: there was a lot of drugs and some scary situations. But recently, he had decided to change. God was calling him to something different and he wanted to come to my church.

Of course, my friend was welcome at my church, and I sat with him every time he came. But the years had affected him, and he felt very out of place in my upper-middle-class professional suburban Bible church. He felt that people were looking at him funny (maybe they were). People asked me about him.

Have you ever felt that way in a church? Jesus started the church as a party, but somewhere along the lines, his followers started writing "formal attire required" on the invitations. Many churches are no longer places where it is safe to let your hair down.

I have another friend whom some might describe as "rough around the edges." He is a Christian, and he said to me one time, "I never struggle with knowing that God loves me, but sometimes I wonder if he *likes* me—like if he were here right now that he'd want to hang out with me."

That thought resonates with me because I have often wondered the same thing (though I never would have been able to put it into words like he did). Does God *like* me? If I invited Jesus over to my house on a Friday night to drink whiskey and play a nerdy board game, would he show up? If he did, would he have a good time?

Yes and yes.

Jesus knows how to party, and he *likes* you. The kingdom of God is a great banquet that he is throwing for *you*.

So, if you haven't yet, respond to that invitation. Come to the banquet table. Every excuse for rejecting God's invitation is poor. It took me years of wearing glasses 24/7 before I broke down and got contacts. I should have gotten them years before I did. I needed them, but I came up with all kinds of excuses not to get them. My glasses work just fine. Contacts are too expensive. I'll get them next year. You know the real reason I didn't get them? I was scared. I was scared of putting something in my eye. The thought freaked me out. But I finally made myself do it, and now I wish I had done it sooner.

In the same way, we come up with all kinds of excuses for not following Jesus. I'm too young. I need to know for sure that there is a God. There are too many hypocrites in church. But when it comes down to it, the real reason we reject God's invitation is because we are afraid. Following Jesus is scary. I've been following for forty years and it's still scary. But it's worth it.

The table is set, the wine is poured, and *you* are the guest of honor. Join Jesus at his table.

QUESTIONS FOR REFLECTION

1. What was the best party you ever attended? What made it so amazing?

2. What do you think the banquet in Jesus' story was like? Think of the preparations and the expense, and think about the guest list. What kinds of things do you think you would have seen had you attended?

3. What is your immediate reaction to the thought that Jesus was accused of being a glutton and a drunkard?

4. If you could have a day to hang out with Jesus, what would you do?

5. What are the scariest parts of accepting Jesus's call to follow him?

6. What can we do to make following Jesus more of a celebration?

Show Tunes

"And whoever gives one of these little ones even a cup of cold water because he is a disciple, truly, I say to you, he will by no means lose his reward." (Matthew 10:42)

I've heard that the most common regret people have at life's end is that they wish they had taken more risks. I believe it. How often do we play it safe and then spend the rest of lives wondering "what if?"

I would have a lot more "what ifs" in my life if it weren't for Jeremy and the stunt he pulled back in high school.

Some people take risks naturally. Others have to be encouraged. I had to be forced. Jeremy used the internet to force me out of my comfort zone and to teach me the value of throwing caution to the wind. It's true what they say about the internet—once you put something out there, it's out there for everyone to see—*everyone*.

I was pretty timid in high school. In fact, to say that I was shy is like saying that Tucker Carlson has some opinions. You've never met anyone as reserved as I am, which is strange since both of my parents had histories in show business. My mom sang like an angel and my dad was a gazelle on the piano. They met in the lounge scene, fell in love, and married. When I came along, they left their music careers for something more stable.

My mom never lost her love for singing, and when my dad died, music soothed the pain. She taught me to sing, and the two of us would retreat to the studio for hours for melodic reprieve. It was during this time of healing that I discovered my gift. I had inherited my father's ear and my mother's range. Sadly, I didn't receive their charisma or love for the stage. I liked to sing, but never for an audience. But that was okay for my mom. "Austin," she'd say. "Your voice is your own. Don't sing for anyone but yourself."

My mom was gracious. She wanted me to chase *my* dreams, not hers. Besides, the bitter aftertaste of show business lingered on her tongue, and she didn't want that life for me. Despite my fear and my mom's warnings, there was a part of me that *did* long for the spotlight. When my thoughts wandered, they took me to sold-out arenas with throngs of imaginary fans. But my dreams stayed just that—dreams. I was too afraid ever to audition for a school play or to join a choir or a band. Instead, I opted for the safer route. My love for the stage led me to several technical teams—set-up and tear-down parties and audio-visual crews.

It was this draw to the stage that got me in trouble. I stayed late at school one day after drama rehearsal to straighten up the dressing room. You see, I *thought* I was alone, and I got caught up in the work, and, well, I started to sing. I wasn't just singing *any* songs—I was singing show tunes. The magic of the theater and costumes and props hypnotized me and brought forth the melodies of the stage. I probably sang for twenty minutes, finishing with an impassioned rendition of *Grease's* "Beauty School Drop-out," when I turned around and saw my friends watching me with glee. Worst of all, my best friend Jeremy was filming the whole thing. They saw the look of horror in my eyes and erupted in mock applause and laughter.

"Bravo!" Jeremy yelled, lowering his phone.

"H—How long have you guys been standing there?"

"Long enough," laughed Jeremy. "You know, you really should be on Broadway." The others burst into a new round of laughter.

"You didn't record that, did you?"

"Just the last song," he said with a smile. "Beauty school drop-out..." he began to sing.

"Give me the phone," I demanded, charging at him with my arm held out.

"No way!" he shouted, dodging me and holding the device aloft. "This is good stuff!"

Jeremy and I had been friends since elementary school. He was always the first to celebrate with me, and he stuck by me when things were tough. But he was also a ham. He chided me for my shyness, but I knew that deep down he had my best at heart.

This stunt was typical of Jeremy. He liked to put me in uncomfortable situations, and he got me good here. I panicked as my mind reviewed what I had done during that song. I had *no idea* I was being watched, so I sang my heart out; I even closed my eyes and gestured wildly. If anyone ever saw that video... "I'm serious. You *have* to delete that video," I begged him.

"Come on, Austin. This could be your ticket to stardom," he mused. The others laughed along. What could I do? This was awful.

"Jeremy, please..." was all I could say.

"Okay, okay," Jeremy finally gave in. "Don't cry about it." He messed with the phone, pushed a couple of buttons, and then he looked up at me. "There. It's gone. Happy?"

"Yes. Thanks. Why were you guys spying on me? That was messed up."

"Sorry, man," Jeremy assured me. "You just looked so happy belting away those tunes. I didn't want to take that away from you. We didn't mean to make you feel uncomfortable. What are you ashamed of, anyway? You have a great voice."

"That's not the point, Jeremy. The point is I wasn't singing for you. You shouldn't have been spying on me."

"Wow. *Sorry.* I didn't realize you were so sensitive. Do you want us to beg you for forgiveness?"

"That would be a start," I said indignantly.

My friends apologized for spying on me and insisted they weren't trying to be mean. I believed them, but I was still embarrassed. I decided it would be best to forget the whole thing and pretend it never happened. So that's what I did. I told myself not to think about it, and I didn't—at least not at first.

***

A week after the singing incident, I was checking my socials and I noticed a message from my friend Luke. It said, "Saw your video!" Fire emojis ensued.

What was he talking about? What video? I hadn't made any videos since... he couldn't be talking about *Jeremy's* video, could he? A shiver ran down my body as I considered the possibility. Surely not. Jeremy wouldn't do that to me.

But he *did* do that to me. I went to Jeremy's page and saw the link to a new video he had posted on YouTube. I clicked the link and was taken to a movie simply called, "Beauty School Drop-out." I gasped. This couldn't be happening. How could he do this to me?

Frantic now, I started to think about how I could survive this crisis. Realistically, how many people would see this video? I mean, it was just one video posted by one guy. How many people could Jeremy possibly know? I looked at the YouTube statistics. Twenty people had viewed the video. Maybe it wasn't too late to get it taken down. I grabbed my phone and gave Jeremy a call.

He answered after the first ring. "Hello?" he asked.

"How could you?!" I shouted. "You told me you deleted that video. How did it get on YouTube?"

Jeremy was silent for a few seconds. "Yeah, I lied about deleting the video. I watched it later and realized how fantastic it was. Austin, you have nothing to be embarrassed—"

"Are you kidding me?" I shouted into the phone. "Nothing to be embarrassed about? I was singing a show tune. I had my eyes closed. I was dancing. Which of those things isn't embarrassing?"

"Austin, have you watched the video?" Jeremy asked. "Your voice is awesome. So, it's goofy. That's not the end of the world." I could tell he was trying hard not to laugh. "I'm telling you, your voice is amazing. I had no idea you could sing like that. Why don't you ever sing for people?"

"That's none of your business," I scolded him. "I don't sing for others, and I certainly don't want anybody to see this video. Take it down."

Jeremy paused. "Sorry, bro," he finally said. "I'm not going to do that. You need this. Why are you always so scared to put yourself out there?"

"I am not joking about this. You're supposed to be my friend. Take it down, or I will never speak to you again."

"Austin, I *am* your friend," Jeremy insisted. "That's why I am not going to take the video down. I think it will be good for you."

I hung up the phone and threw it across the room. What a backstabbing jerk. I couldn't believe he would do this to me and then still insist that he was my friend. Had he no concept of what a friend was?

I collapsed into a chair and buried my face in my hands. I wasn't going to cry. It wasn't worth it. But this was awful. How many people were going to see this? One hundred? Two hundred?

I had no idea how wrong I was.

***

The next day, I went to school with a mixture of anger and apprehension. I couldn't wait to find Jeremy. What would I do to him? Would I kill him, or just maim him? At the same time, I was terrified—terrified at who may have seen the video.

I walked in the front door of my school, and instantly felt everyone's stares. People smiled as I walked past them. Some whispered as they pointed me out to their friends. Was I imagining this, or was everyone laughing at me?

I made my way to my locker and fumbled with the combination. Rachel, whose locker was next to mine, showed up and gave me a smile. "Good morning, Austin," she said. "I saw your video. *Hilarious.* I had no idea you could sing."

I dropped my books and looked at her in disbelief. "You saw it?" I asked with a mixture of terror and remorse.

"Yeah," she said. "Lindsey sent me the link."

Lindsey? *She* saw it? Had *everyone* seen it? I shoved my books into my bag, slammed my locker and reached for my phone. I needed to check the video and find out who had seen it.

I opened YouTube and looked for the views. My heart sank at the sight—5,000 views. The video had a ton of upvotes, though, and 200 people had commented on it. I scrolled through the names of the commenters, only recognizing half of them. The comments alternated between "hilarious," "LOL," "awesome," and "what a voice!" "Who is this kid?" "I didn't know Austin could sing."

I lowered my phone and pressed my head against a locker in despair. Everyone in the school had seen it—and they all told friends. For the rest of the year, I was going to be known as the "Beauty School Drop-out" kid. Unbelievable. How could Jeremy have done this to me? He was supposed to be my friend.

***

Jeremy must have skipped school that day, because I never found him. It was a wise move, too. I think I would have wrung his neck had I seen him. When I got home, I called him for an explanation. Jeremy could tell that I was mad, and he insisted we talk about it in person.

He came over later that night. When I heard his car outside, I sprung up and ran toward the door. I yanked it open and huffed out toward him. "I'm going to kill you!" I shouted as I made my way toward him.

Jeremy held out his hands and started backing toward his car. "Hold on there, big guy," he said nervously. "Why kill me? I am trying to help you."

"Help me?" I screamed in disbelief. "By ruining my life?"

"How did I ruin your life?" Jeremy demanded.

"Everyone at school has seen that video, Jeremy. My life is over."

"Everyone *at school*?" Jeremy laughed. "Have you checked the site lately? Everyone *in the world* has seen that video. And your life is far from over."

What? I stood there for a second, and then pulled out my phone. It seemed to crawl as it loaded the video. When it finally showed up, I looked in horror at the number in front of me—two million views. I sat down, dumbfounded. Two *million* views? How could that be? It was just one video posted by one guy. How could the word have spread so fast?

I stared at the screen in disbelief when Jeremy spoke up. "What are we up to?" he asked excitedly. I turned to him, speechless.

"My life is over," I finally said. "How does that make you feel?"

"Your life's not over," he laughed. "Have you read the comments? They love you!"

I looked back at the screen. The video now had 100,000 upvotes, and there were several thousand comments—all positive. Could he be right? Did people actually *like* this?

"Austin, you're acting like I posted this to hurt you. I told you I didn't. I posted it because I knew *you* never would. Your voice is amazing, and this video is going to show that to the world. Sure, it's a little juvenile, but that adds to the appeal. You could really go far with that voice, but you're never going anywhere if you don't step up and take a risk."

A risk? What was he talking about? "Why didn't you ask me first?"

"I knew what you'd say. I knew you'd be scared. Austin, we can spend our whole lives playing it safe. And yeah, we'll never make a mistake that way, but we'll also never do anything great. I think you could be great; you just need some publicity. That's the beauty of the internet. You start with something small—one video posted by one guy, and before you know it the whole world has seen it."

I was pondering this new take on things when my phone rang. I didn't recognize the number, but I answered anyway. "Hello?"

"Hello, Austin?"

"Yeah."

"My name is Arthur Williams. I work for Rising Star Talent Agency. I saw your video on YouTube. Have you ever thought about singing professionally?"

I looked over at Jeremy. He was beaming.

And so, that was my first break. Now, I didn't go on to become rich and famous. I doubt you've ever heard of me. But I *do* sing and write songs now. And yes, people even *pay* to hear me perform. And no, they don't call me the "Beauty School Drop-out" kid—at least not all of the time.

The internet is an amazing thing. You start with something small—one video posted by one kid, and the next thing you know millions of people have seen it.

Sometimes I think about what I would have done if someone told me on the day I was caught singing that millions of people were going to see the video and that it would be my ticket to a successful singing career. Would that have changed my attitude toward putting it online? Would I have been more willing to risk if I knew the results?

Maybe. But when do we ever know the future like that? Never. That's why it's a risk—because we don't know. Maybe you'll be famous; maybe you'll be a laughingstock. But it's the *risks* that make life worth living. Sometimes, you just have to sing your heart out, close your eyes, and click "submit."

"He put another parable before them, saying, 'The kingdom of heaven is like a grain of mustard seed that a man took and sowed in his field. It is the smallest of all seeds, but when it has grown it is larger than all the garden plants and becomes a tree, so that the birds of the air come and make nests in its branches.' He told them another parable. 'The kingdom of heaven is like leaven that a woman took and hid in three measures of flour, till it was all leavened.'" (Matthew 13:31–33)

IN MARK 13, JESUS is walking through Jerusalem with his disciples shortly before his betrayal. As he comes out of the temple, one of his disciples points out the majesty of building and says, "Look, Teacher, what wonderful stones and what wonderful buildings!"[1] They were impressed by the "big" things people did for God.

It is natural for us to look for God in the "big." We look for God in megachurches, international ministries, global movements, and celebrity conversions. We want to change the world.

In Matthew 13:31–33, Jesus tells two stories that challenge this tendency. In parallel parables, he compares the kingdom of God to a mustard seed and a lump of dough. "The mustard seed is the smallest of all seeds," he says, "but it grows into a very large tree." Likewise, a little leaven worked into some dough eventually spreads and leavens the whole lump.

In other words, the kingdom is in the *small*. In the kingdom, the small *becomes* the big.

Contrast the temple with Jesus himself. There was nothing majestic or wonderful about Jesus. He was born under questionable circumstances. We know very little about his childhood. He never wrote a book, never held an office, never won a battle. He had twelve close followers who all abandoned him in his hour of need. He died alone.

If you were a bystander to the cross and saw Christ crucified, there is *no way* you would think, *this is the way God is going to change history.*

And yet.

In the kingdom of God, the small becomes big. Jesus said "Truly, truly, I say to you, unless a grain of wheat falls into the earth and dies, it remains

1. Mark 13:1.

25

alone; but if it dies, it bears much fruit."[2] Jesus's death and resurrection launched God's master plan of redemption and reconciliation. The small becomes big.

In this way, the kingdom of God is like a viral video. Once people start sharing, things take on a life of their own. What started with one share can become ten, then one thousand, then one million.

In 2010, I stepped off an airplane in Cochabamba, Bolivia for the first time. I was traveling with ten other people from my church on a vision trip to explore the possibility of partnering with Food for the Hungry for a decade of work in a distressed community called Ushpa Ushpa.

We were greeted at the airport by children holding welcome banners and homemade signs. In the parking lot outside of the airport they sang us traditional Bolivian welcome songs. Then, we loaded up the vans and set off to begin a decade-long relationship with some wonderful people.

Part of the work with Food for the Hungry involved child sponsorship, and my family sponsored a young girl named Marianne. She was nine at the time. Living in Ushpa Ushpa, Marianne faced an uphill battle. Most homes in the area did not have latrines or clean water. The local school was under-resourced, and children had to travel by public transit up to an hour to reach a library. Abuse and domestic violence were prevalent in her community.

I was able to meet Marianne on my second trip to Bolivia. She lived with her mom and her brother, and when I asked what I could pray for, she asked that I pray her dad would come home. He had been working in Spain and she hadn't seen him in years. The next year, I visited her again and she had the same prayer request: pray that my dad comes home.

The *next* year, I visited her again and she had the *same* request: pray that my dad comes home. After several years of the same prayer request, I started to wonder.

Then one day, he came home.

He had been gone for nine years. She never saw him from age six to fifteen. Then he came home.

Life for Marianne and her family was hard for those years, but they stayed the course. She graduated from high school and then went to medical school to become an OB-GYN and serve the community she grew up in.

I last met her family in 2018. We said goodbye. I brought letters from my kids, and we told her how proud we were of her for making it through

2. John 12:24.

school and how excited we were for her future. I got to pray with her family (including her dad), and it was an emotional goodbye, but a good one. Her kids are going to have a *very different* life than she did.

Like Jesus's disciples, our vision of the kingdom of God often focuses on the big. *What wonderful stones! What wonderful buildings!* But Jesus focuses on the small things, like helping your neighbor build a fence, volunteering at the local food bank, or making meals for the homeless.

Sponsoring a child like Marianne is a simple act of kindness. No one would mistake it for a "big," world-changing act. But in a way, it is. It made a big difference to *her*. That's how the kingdom works—God takes small acts of love and grows them into something huge.

QUESTIONS FOR REFLECTION

1. Have you or a friend ever had a social media post go viral? If so, what was that like?

2. Imagine you were one of Jesus's disciples hearing the parable of the mustard seed for the first time. What would your immediate reaction be?

3. Why do you think so many people are drawn to "big" things? Why is it so hard for us to think "small"?

4. How have you been blessed by someone else's small acts of kindness?

5. What is one way that you wish your community was different? What small acts of kindness could move you toward that vision?

6. What's the first step? What is God calling you to do today?

Insurance

"[Cast] all your anxieties on him, because he cares for you."
(1 Peter 5:7)

Sarah leaned her back against the open front door of her suburban Georgia home so that her twelve-year-old son, Cason could crutch his way into the house. His backpack over one of her shoulders, and her arms full of groceries and the daily mail, she was struggling to make into the house herself.

What a day, she thought to herself. *Now I have to figure out what to make for dinner.*

Tuesdays were one of Cason's physical therapy days. Ever since he was released from the hospital following the accident, her son had to do rigorous physical therapy three days per week. It pained her to watch her son struggle through the exercises, but it was the quickest path forward to walking without the crutches.

"Get a start on your homework," she reminded Cason as she made her way into the kitchen. "There's not much free time today because of the PT." Sarah laid the groceries down on the kitchen counter, set Cason's backpack on the table, and turned her attention to the mail.

Aside from the physical therapy, sorting through the mail was the toughest part of the day. They still hadn't settled with the insurance company of the man who hit Cason with his car. "Peace of Mind Insurance" they called themselves. She sure wasn't experiencing any peace of mind.

It had been months since that man struck her son with his car. Hospital bills remained unpaid and now physical therapy bills were piling up. Peace of Mind Insurance was fighting her at every turn. First, they told her that she didn't need to file with them because she had her own health insurance.

If there was anything worse than arguing with an insurance company, it was arguing with *two* insurance companies about *who* should pay.

When Cason was in the hospital, she *should have* had the freedom to give him her undivided attention. Instead, she had to sit by his bed and make phone calls to try to get Peace of Mind to pay for the massive medical bills her son was racking up.

She spent so much time on the phone, she was on a first-name basis with the rep handling her claim—Jim Montgomery. She rolled her eyes and sighed deeply even thinking about him. *A robot would be more compassionate*, she thought.

The day's mail included the usual—advertisements for realtors, and coupons for the local grocery store, and then there came the part she dreaded. Notice from a doctor. A separate notice from the hospital—this one was addressed in red font. Red font was never good on a bill.

Her stomach sank as she flipped through the bills. *I will deal with these later*, she thought. There was no money to pay them, anyway.

When she got to the bottom of the stack, she saw something that made her eyes light up—it was from Peace of Mind Insurance. It looked like a check.

She tore the envelope open and read the contents furiously. It was from Jim Montgomery from Peace of Mind.

"Dear Ms. Cunningham," it began. "We have been evaluating your claim, and while we maintain that our client was not at fault, we are willing to settle with you for the enclosed amount. By depositing the check, you are agreeing to drop your claim against Mr. Craig and against Peace of Mind Insurance."

She stopped reading and looked at the enclosed check.

$10,000.

It was a lot of money, but not enough to cover the hospital bills, let alone the doctors and the physical therapy. This would not do. They were trying to get out of paying the full amount.

How could they think they could do this to her family?

How could they possibly think that the accident wasn't their client's fault?

He was in a car and her son was on a bike. What else mattered?

Jim Montgomery's direct line was on the letter. She grabbed for her cell phone and began punching in the numbers to settle this right now.

The phone rang twice before it was answered. "Hello, this is Jim," the voice on the other end answered.

"Jim, this is Sarah Cunningham. I just got your 'settlement' in the mail. How could you?"

"Hello, Ms. Cunningham," the voice at the other end of the phone responded coldly. "I am glad you received our offer. I hope this can put to rest the matter between us."

"Put to rest?" She could feel her temperature rising. "How could it put it to rest? Ten thousand dollars won't even pay the *hospital* bills, let alone everything else. How do you sleep at night doing things like this?"

"I am not sure what you mean, Ms. Cunningham. We feel our offer is extremely generous, seeing that our client was not responsible for the accident. We just want to move on."

"Move on? Jim, do you have kids?"

"I am not sure how that is relevant," he responded.

"Have you ever had to see your child in a hospital bed and not be sure he will wake up? Have you ever had to see him struggle through physical therapy? Have you ever had to live with the guilt of weighing treatments because you aren't sure what you can *pay* for? How is this bringing 'Peace of Mind'?"

"Ms. Cunningham, what happened to your son is unfortunate, but I can't make decisions based on sad stories. My job is to honor the insurance agreement I have with my client. In this particular case, that doesn't mean offering *you* anything. I advise you to cash the check and leave us alone."

"Absolutely not," Sarah said adamantly. "This is not the last you will hear from me."

She hung up without waiting for Montgomery's response.

Sarah stood there in the kitchen, steaming. She was starting to hate insurance companies. How could they refuse to pay her claim? As she stewed, she looked over at her son, who was *supposed* to be working on his homework at the kitchen table. Instead, he was looking at her, sad.

"It's okay," she said. "We're going to be okay. I am sorry you had to hear that. We will figure this out. In the meantime, I don't feel like cooking tonight. How would you feel about pizza?"

A smile came over Cason's face and his eyes lit up.

***

Three weeks later, Sarah was at physical therapy with Cason per their routine. *He* was making progress, but *she* was not. Peace of Mind was not budging on their position. She sat in a chair against the wall and watched her son struggle to stretch his legs with the therapist across the exercise center, when an office worker approached her with a clipboard in hand and an awkward smile on her face.

"Ms. Cunningham?" she asked nervously.

"Yes, that's me."

"Hi. I am Angela with billing. Do you have a minute?"

She had an hour. "Yes, of course. What's up?"

"Well, I was just curious how things were going with your insurance. We still waiting for payments."

"Well, it's not *my* insurance," Sarah interrupted. "He was hit by a car and the guy's insurance company is refusing to pay."

"Oh, I am sorry about that," Angela said superficially. "Do you have a timeline on when all of this will be resolved? The bills are all past due. We want to continue to see Cason, but we won't be able to if his account isn't paid."

Sarah's heart sank. She knew this day was coming. "We're working on it. I am in touch with them almost every day. I don't know what else to do—they are supposed to pay for all of this."

"Yes, I am sorry." Angela said awkwardly. "Unfortunately, if we don't get something from them by the end of the month, we won't be able to continue to see Cason. But I can refer you to some other centers who might be able to help."

Sarah's heartbeat began to pick up. "I will call them *right now*," Sarah said. Angela smiled again, sadly, and walked away.

Sarah called Jim Montgomery—no need to look up his number this time; she had added him as a contact.

"Hello, this is Jim," the familiar voice answered on the other end.

"Jim, this is Sarah Cunningham."

A sigh on the other end. "Yes, Ms. Cunningham. How can I help you *today*?" The way he emphasized "today" made Sarah seethe inside.

"I want an update on my appeal. Where do we stand? The physical therapist is threatening to cut us off. *They* need to be paid and *you* need to pay them."

"Well, we received your appeal, and there seems to be some discrepancies. We're going to need you to send us Cason's medical records. We just need to make sure that all of his treatments are due to the accident and not some other preexisting condition."

"A preexisting condition?!" Sarah asked incredulously. "Like he got hit by a different car first?! This is ridiculous. I don't want to have to take legal action against you, but you are leaving me few other options."

"I would discourage that," Jim said. "We will win this in court. Send us his records and we will evaluate your appeal."

"Are you going to be able to do this before the end of the month? The physical therapists need to be paid by the end of the month."

"That is out of my hands," Jim said coldly. "Send us the records and we will see what happens."

Sarah hung up the phone and tears began to form in her eyes.

***

It was a welcome relief when Sarah's friend Christy invited her out to coffee the next day. With so much going on, Sarah needed the advice of a friend. Christy was a good listener and always had good thoughts.

"I don't know what I am going to do," she said as she sat down with her latte. "The insurance company refuses to help me."

"How can they do that?" asked Christy.

"Well, they keep changing their story. First, they tried to get me to use my health insurance. But his injuries were the result of a *car* accident. Then, they rejected my claims saying that it wasn't clear that their client was at fault. Then they tried to settle with me for an amount that wouldn't cover my bills. Now, they are overwhelming me with paperwork requests. They are saying that they need his full medical history."

"Yeah, they don't need that," Christy interrupted. "That's a scam. They are just looking for an excuse not to pay out."

"So, what do I do?" Sarah asked. "How do I get them to pay? I am running out of time here. The physical therapists are saying that if they don't get paid by the end of the month that they can't continue to see Cason. What do I do?"

Christy hesitated. "Have you considered hiring an attorney? That might be the only thing they respond to."

Sarah shook her head. "I have thought of that," she said. "But I am overwhelmed with bills already. How could I add attorney fees on top of everything else? Plus, they seem pretty confident they would win in court."

Christy reached across the table and took her hand. "I am so sorry, Sarah. This shouldn't be happening to you."

"Thank you. I'm not going to give up," she continued. "Cason is just a kid. He can't fight for himself, and he deserves someone to fight *for* him. I am not going to give up until he gets the care he needs—whatever it costs me."

Christy nodded her head in agreement. "Have you ever considered one of those crowdsourcing platforms? You could get your story out and others could help you fund the attorney fees."

"I hadn't considered that," Sarah admitted. "Do you think that would work?"

"I think it would," Christy said. "In fact, I think you should do as much as possible to get your story out. I think people will get behind you and possibly put some pressure on the insurance company. Oh, have you considered contacting the media?"

"The media? Like, the news?"

"Yes!" Christy said, lighting up. "I would love to help you with this. Why don't you set up the crowdsourcing page and I will contact the media. I will try to get a newsperson to contact you about telling your story."

"You'd do that that for me?" Sarah asked.

"Of course!"

"Do you think this will work?"

"I do!" Christy insisted. "Here, I will send you a link to the crowdsourcing website."

***

The next week was exhilarating for Sarah. For the first time since her son's accident, she felt empowered. While Peace of Mind still hadn't paid, she was starting to think that she could pressure them to do it. Crowdsourcing had *worked*—her friends, family, and even strangers had heard her story, donated to her legal fund, and reached out to her in support.

Physical therapy was also going well. Cason was making real progress and Sarah was beginning to think that he would make a full recovery. The bills were still piling up, and she still only had one more week to pay for therapy, but for the first time she had hope.

She was dwelling on this hope at physical therapy when her cell phone rang. She looked at the screen and saw the name of the caller—Jim Montgomery from Peace of Mind Insurance.

Sarah's stomach tightened. Could this be the call?

"Hello?" she answered.

"Hello, Mrs. Cunningham? This is Jim Montgomery from Peace of Mind Insurance. Do you have a minute?"

"Yes. Hello, Jim. I do have a minute. I am just here at physical therapy with my son. Do you have good news for me?"

There was silence on the other end until Jim eventually spoke up. "Mrs. Cunningham, we heard from your attorney."

"Oh, good," Sarah smiled. "What did he say?"

"Well, he informed us of your lawsuit. We also heard from a news anchor asking us about our situation."

"That's wonderful," Sarah responded.

"Yes, well, it is really unfortunate that you have taken these steps."

"You're right it's unfortunate," Sarah interrupted. "I tried everything I could to get you to pay. You refused to listen. This was the only step I could take to get you to take responsibility."

Again, silence on the other end of the phone.

Eventually Jim spoke up. "We were hoping we would be able to settle with you privately considering that our client is not at fault."

Sarah could barely contain her laughter. "Not at fault?! Your client was in a car and my son was on a bike! How could he not be at fault?"

"Well," Jim responded. "You will be hearing our case from our attorney. The fact of the matter is your son should not have been at that crosswalk in the first place. That trail is for walkers, not bikers."

Sarah was flabbergasted. "What—" she began.

"Your son was not following the laws of the road. He should not have been biking that trail and our client should not have had to anticipate a bike at that crosswalk. In fact, we will make the case that you are liable to the damage done to our client's car."

Now it was Sarah's time to be silent.

Finally, she spoke up. "I can't believe what I am hearing right now. I can't believe that you actually believe this. Do you not care about the time my kid spent in the hospital?"

"Ma'am, it is not my job to care about sob stories. I am just interested in the facts, and the fact is that your son was at fault."

Sarah hung up the phone in disbelief.

***

The phone call with Jim took the wind out of Sarah's sails. The next week was not the same high as the week before. Time was running out, and things seemed to be going from bad to worse.

She returned from physical therapy with her son again, as she had multiple times per week for months since the accident.

Helping Cason to the table to start his homework, she commenced the daily chore of sifting through the mail.

Bills from the hospital.

Bills from the doctor.

Bills from the therapist. Several marked "final notice."

Tears began to form in her eyes as she struggled through plans to pay for everything. Nothing came to mind.

As she was reflecting, her phone rang. This time she was not excited. This time, she dreaded to see the number on the other end.

She glanced at her phone.

It was Christy.

At least she had a friend to share her pain with.

"Hi Christy," she answered her phone.

"Have you seen your social feed?!" she blurted.

"What?" Sarah responded.

"Go online. Right now." Christy insisted. "Your story has gone viral."

"W-what do you mean? H-How did this happen?" Sarah was speechless.

"The news story. I told you I contacted the media. They ran your story with a link to your fundraising page. There are *thousands* of comments on the page. People are dunking on the insurance company and dropping their policies. It's amazing!"

Sarah hung up, logged on, and found the article about her case. Sure enough, sympathetic voice after sympathetic voice was expressing outrage over how her family was treated by Peace of Mind. Calls to boycott the company and links to alternate insurance companies threaded through the comment section.

The feeling of hope was beginning to return. Maybe she *could* get through to Peace of Mind. Maybe she *could* get justice.

Sarah wasn't dwelling with these thoughts long before her phone rang again. This time it wasn't Christy.

It was Jim Montgomery.

Sarah gained her composure and answered the phone with as much gravity as she could muster. "Hello, Jim," she said matter-of-factly.

"Ms. Cunningham. Do you have a moment?"

"I do," she said somewhat more cheerfully.

"I am sure by now you have seen the stories online about your case."

"Yes, I have," she responded.

"Well. You have won. It is unfortunate that it has come to this, but we have decided that it would be more expensive for us to fight for the truth than it would be just to pay out your case. So, we are willing to do that. We will pay the medical bills, the therapy bills, and other expenses you have incurred if you go back to the news and tell them that there was a misunderstanding and that we have been responsive to your case. Your son will get the care he needs."

A smile spread over Sarah's face. She heard him say it. She had won.

"And he told them a parable to the effect that they ought always to pray and not lose heart. He said, 'In a certain city there was a judge who neither feared God nor respected man. And there was a widow in that city who kept coming to him and saying, "Give me justice against my adversary." For a while he refused, but afterward he said to himself, "Though I neither fear God nor respect man, yet because this widow keeps bothering me, I will give her justice, so that she will not beat me down by her continual coming." And the Lord said, 'Hear what the unrighteous judge says. And will not God give justice to his elect, who cry to him day and night? Will he delay long over them? I tell you, he will give justice to them speedily. Nevertheless, when the Son of Man comes, will he find faith on earth?'" (Luke 18:1–8)

IN 1 SAMUEL 1, there is a story about a woman named Hannah who desperately wants a child. Her rival, Peninnah, flaunts her own fertility and constantly reminds Hannah that she is childless. Hannah is so upset about it that she refuses to eat. Her husband tries to affirm his love for her, but it doesn't fill the hole of infertility.

One day, Hannah is in the temple praying about her situation. The text says she is "deeply distressed and prayed to the Lord and wept bitterly."[1] The priest Eli sees her praying, and her behavior is so intense that he mistakes her for being drunk.

Have you ever prayed so fervently that anyone who saw you would mistake you for being drunk?

There are times in life when you pray, and then there are times in life when you *pray*. What I mean by this is that there are times when you casually pray for things and then there are times when you *pray* with deep distress and intensity.

Hannah prayed with intensity for years, and for years God was silent. Then one day, God answered Hannah's prayer and enabled her to conceive. The Scriptures say "And Elkanah knew Hannah his wife, and the LORD remembered her. And in due time Hannah conceived and bore a son, and

---

1. 1 Samuel 1:10.

she called his name Samuel, for she said, 'I have asked for him from the LORD.'"[2]

The Scriptures say the Lord "remembered" Hannah. The Hebrew word used in 1 Samuel 1:19 is *zachar*, which is often used for God "remembering" his people and answering their prayers after long periods of silence.[3]

In Luke 18, Jesus tells a story that speaks to God's silence. In his story, a widow goes to a judge for vindication against her adversary. Jesus tells us that the judge neither feared God nor cared about men (he *should have* done both). At first, the judge refuses to give her justice. Eventually, like a woman persisting with an insurance company, the widow wears the unjust judge down with her perseverance.

The parable uses what we call in Latin an a fortiori argument—"from the lesser to the greater." In other words, the point of the parable is *not* that God is like an unjust judge or like a disinterested insurance company, but rather that because God *does* care for us, *how much more* will he grant us justice when we pray.

God cares for you. He *hears* you.

Never stop praying. The Scriptures tell us that God hears us, but his timing is not always our timing. Peter reminds us: "But do not overlook this one fact, beloved, that with the Lord one day is as a thousand years, and a thousand years as one day."[4]

Never give up praying. God cares and he hears.

I will never forget the night on which my oldest son was born, because on that night I *prayed*. Zack was a big baby, and there was a long time during his birth when the doctors could not detect his vital signs. When he was finally delivered, he was blue and lifeless. He scored a one out of ten on the Apgar test.

As soon as he was born, the nurses pulled the code alarm and medical professionals of all kinds flooded the room. As they intubated him, I started to pray. It was one of those times when I *prayed*.

"Lord, please let my son live" is a different kind of prayer than most prayers. When I prayed it, none of the other worries in my life mattered.

After intubation, my son's color began to return. Eventually, he moved. Then he opened his eyes. Then, he tried to remove the breathing tube on his

2. 1 Samuel 1:19–20.

3. Genesis 30:22; Exodus 2:24; Judges 16:28.

4. 2 Peter 3:8.

own and, when they finally pulled it out, he *cried*. It was the most beautiful sound I had ever heard.

We had already planned on naming our son Zachary, but the name fits. It's an Americanized version of the Hebrew Zechariah: "The Lord remembers me." It's derived from that Hebrew word *zachar*. I will never forget that day I prayed, and the Lord remembered me.

Sometimes, it feels like God is absent or that he is silent. I assure you—he is there and he cares.

Never stop praying.

QUESTIONS FOR REFLECTION

1. Have you ever had to pester someone to do the right thing? What was the situation and how did it resolve?

2. What is your initial reaction to Jesus' story? How did the judge's attitude make you feel?

3. Have there been times in your life when God seemed absent or silent?

4. How does it feel to pray for something and not receive an answer?

5. Do you agree that there is a difference between praying for something and *praying* for something (with intensity)? Can you think of examples of each in your life?

6. What is one way you can remind yourself that God cares for you and hears your prayers?

Helix

"Far be it from me to boast except in the cross of our Lord Jesus Christ." (Galatians 6:14)

It's been said that how we spend our days is how we spend our lives. What you are doing with this hour or that one is what you are doing with your life. What I was doing on that day was wandering. But all that changed when I met Rustin.

I met him at a job fair of all places. I was nearing the end of my senior year, and I still didn't have any leads for life after college. As it turns out, employers aren't lined up to hire computer science majors with 2.1 GPAs and skills in keg stands, video games, and binging anime. Yeah, I probably could have done better in school, but that seriously would have cut into my hanging out time. Besides, I had Helix. Who needs grades when you have an idea that's going to change the world?

Helix was a computer operating system that my buddies and I developed between rounds of pool and episodes of Battlestar Galactica. It started as an open-source thing, but as we got going, we decided it was too good to trust to the public. This was our DOS, our Facebook, our big idea that was going to make us all millions one day.

Or so we thought. As it turns out, programs like this aren't easy to develop. They take time. They take failure, revision, and patience. And who has time for patience—especially when rent is due next Tuesday.

So, when I met Rustin, Helix was in the can, and I was looking for a real job. But the prospects weren't what I thought they'd be. Everyone at this stupid fair was the stiff corporate type—power tie, fake tan, cheesy smile—you know the look. And let's face it, I didn't have the corporate look. Admittedly, I shouldn't have worn my Family Guy T-shirt (you know, the one with Stewie Griffon posing like Al Pacino in Scarface), but laundry day wasn't until the weekend, and I didn't have many other options.

So I was lingering by this booth for a company called Atlas or Zeus or something like that, reading a brochure about company goals, core values, and employment prospects. The guy behind the booth with the fake tan was being polite and asking me about my future plans, but we both knew that I wasn't going to end up at Atlas. Or was it Zeus? Anyway, it didn't matter. I gave the guy my email address and started to back away from the booth.

But as I stepped away, I bumped into this guy who looked like he just got off the beach. He had light, shaggy brown hair and a wicked goatee. When I saw his cutoffs and flip flops, I suddenly didn't feel so bad about my choice of attire.

"'Scuse me, bro." he said, smiling as he checked out my less-than-professional get-up. "I like your shirt. Best movie ever. And Stewie looks the part."

"Thanks," I said, cautiously. Who was this guy, and what was he doing at the job fair? He was too old to be a student; he looked like he was like thirty-five or something. But the casual attire probably meant he wasn't considering hiring anyone. He appeared more like a washed-up front man for a surf rock band. And yet, there was something about him that intrigued me. He had a presence, a charisma, an aura about him that was both commanding and disarming at the same time.

"I'm Rustin," he said, extending his hand. "Rustin Maddock."

"Brian Carter," I responded, shaking his hand hesitantly.

"How's the search going?" he asked, motioning to the brochure in my hand.

"Pretty good," I lied. "I've got some leads."

"I don't mean to be rude," he said, "but you don't exactly look the corporate type. Do you seriously think you're going to find something here?"

I was taken back. "Well, a job's a job. Besides, I just need something to pay the bills while my friends and I finish Helix...." I stopped short as I realized what I had just said. I couldn't believe I was telling this guy about my project. It was nowhere near done. In fact, it was quite laughable at this stage.

"Helix? What's that?" His eyebrows perked as he asked. Something I said must have interested him.

"Well, it's an operating system," I said more confidently. "It's going to be huge. My friends and I have been developing it for a couple years now." I then went on to describe the scope of the project and how Helix was going to change the way we think about PCs. Again, I don't know what came over me or why I was telling this guy I didn't know about my idea. I felt like an octogenarian showing some poor stranger wallet-sized pictures of my grandkids while we waited for the bus. But he was eating it up. He asked good questions and seemed genuinely interested.

"Brian, I want to make a deal with you," he finally said. "I like you and I think you might be on to something with this Helix thing."

"Go on..."

"I own a small software company, and I want to hire you to develop Helix for me."

"Seriously?" I asked.

"Yeah. I will fund the entire project. I will pay you a salary as you develop it, and when you're done, I own the finished project. If it bombs, I'm out of my investment. But if it's as good as you say it's going to be, then I make some money. How's that sound?"

I was still in shock over the idea that someone would pay me to work on Helix. Was this guy out of his mind? He had no evidence that my project was worth *anything*. And while I hated the idea of losing the rights to Helix, I had to admit his offer sounded pretty good. He would *completely* fund my project. That took away all of the risk and all of the headache. Besides, even if the project tanked, I could put the work on my resume.

"Well, I don't think I could finish it without my friends. It's been a team project up to this—"

"Say no more," he interrupted. "They're hired, too. We need some more programmers. What do you say?"

"Well, I'll ask them about it. How big is your company, anyway? How many guys do you have working for you?"

"Including you? One."

I laughed. "Why would you do this?" I asked.

"Because about ten years ago I was at one of these fairs just like you. I was looking for a break and someone took a chance on me. I made some money and now I am looking to pay it forward."

Sounded good to me.

***

So that was that. I pitched Rustin's idea to my friends, and they were ecstatic. None of us was excited about working in a cube somewhere, anyway. Six months later, we were on the job. We were realizing a common dream. But I don't think any of us was prepared for the ride we were about to take.

Rustin's "company" actually operated out of the basement of his house. He set up a couple of folding tables and some makeshift workstations. The whole thing felt like Wayne's World meets Hewlett Packard. We called it the dungeon. But we had a pool table and an Xbox and a refrigerator. What more could you ask for?

My friends and I spent the next couple of years making Helix a reality. The job was hard, but I loved working with my friends, and I couldn't have asked for a better boss. Rustin paid us way more than we deserved. He was generous with time off and he never complained about setbacks. Sometimes he would even stop by to challenge us to a game of 9-ball or Halo. He was easily the coolest boss ever.

One day Rustin came downstairs into the dungeon with a spark in his eyes and a spring in his step. He was always pretty upbeat, but I had never seen him like this.

"Guess what I am holding in my hands?" He asked, displaying the latest issue of *PC Magazine*.

"Looks like a magazine," I said, pointing out the obvious.

"Good eyes. But it is not just a magazine, it's this month's issue of *PC Magazine*, and they've reviewed Helix. Wanna read with me?"

Did we ever. We had just finished the project and Rustin had sent it to some of his connections in the industry to play around with and review. One of them must have worked for *PC*.

Rustin began to read the review. "From page 63: 'Helix amazes in functionality, simplicity, and style. 9.5 out of 10.'"

He stopped. We all looked at each other in shock. This was going to be huge. Rustin continued with the rest of the article. It gushed. It was the highest-rated product by the magazine that year. When he had finished, he tossed the magazine and threw his arms around us in an over-enthusiastic group hug. He looked like he was going to jump right out of his skin. The rest of us didn't know what to do. I mean, we thought that our project was good, but I don't think any of us really expected *this*. I mean, *PC Magazine*? They had subscribers all over the globe. This was going to be huge. There is no way our website was going to be able to handle all of the downloads.... oh man, the website!

"Guys, has anyone checked the website since this article went out?" No one had. We tried to load it on my computer and, sure enough, it was down. Too much traffic. Helix had gone public, and it was bigger than we could handle.

"We need to expand," said Rustin. "Say goodbye to the dungeon. We need more space. And we need to hire some more people. Now that the world has seen our work, they're going to find bugs. We're going to need a quick turnaround on updates and support."

***

So, Helix was alive and well. We had a real product on our hands. But that was just the beginning. Helix was about to get bigger.

Two months after release, we were working out of an office space down the street. Just like he said, Rustin went out and hired some more guys. They were good, and it really helped the workload. Still, with the new demand, we had to put some more hours in. But we all got raises and better job titles and nicer equipment. It sure beat working in the dungeon.

It's funny, despite all the hype I gave Helix, deep down I never expected it to succeed. Honestly, I saw myself working in Rustin's basement for a couple of months before we all just packed it in, gave up, and looked for real jobs. But we made it happen!

And so now, just a few years after I met Rustin at the job fair, here I was in a rented office space, sitting in a cube, working for a software company. And our flagship product was the one I started in college. This was everything I wanted in life.

After working out of the rented office space for a couple months, Rustin called me into his office one day. "Brian," he said, "I have good news for you."

"What is it?" I asked.

"We're going retail," he said. "Wal-Mart, Target, Costco, they all want to sell Helix. I've just worked a deal with a distributor. I wanted you to be the first to know."

We both sat there in silence for about a minute as he let the significance of this announcement sink in. The traffic on our website had been overwhelming since we released Helix. But all of that traffic was nothing compared to the sales we would get by putting Helix in a box and selling it at Wal-Mart. Rustin was going to make millions. And I couldn't have been happier for him. He took a huge risk in hiring us, and he stuck with us for years as we trudged through the process of realizing our dream for Helix. All along we had steady paychecks, health insurance, and the best work environment you could ask for.

"Congratulations, Rustin. You deserve this," I said. "I am happy for you."

"Thanks," he said. "You know, none of this would have happened if it weren't for you. The idea was yours. I just financed it. This is a big day for you, too. You should be proud. It's quite a program you put together."

And he was right. It was a big day for me. I had put Helix together, and I'm not too humble to admit that, in fact, it *was* a great program. It's what the world needed.

***

Two years later, you wouldn't have recognized any of us. Gone were the jeans and T-shirts. Rustin said that we were a real business now and we needed to look the part. He even ditched the cutoffs and flip flops and started sporting a tie. We had to hire more staff to meet the new demands of going retail. We had a marketing team, a call center help desk, and an HR department. We moved to this funky new office downtown made from a renovated warehouse. It had a great industrial look with contemporary art on the walls in the hallways. We even had to hire a receptionist to handle all of the traffic coming and going from the office.

I was reflecting on these changes as I made my way to the office one day. Five years ago, I didn't have much going on. Now here I was, stable job with my own office, doing what I love to do. Yeah, life was good. I sat down at my computer and browsed through the morning emails. There was a message flagged urgent in my inbox from Rustin himself. It was sent to everyone in the company and the body of the message simply said. "Major announcement today at 2:00 in Conference Room B. Be there."

What could this be about? I phoned the receptionist, but she didn't know. No one knew. The whole office was abuzz with speculation—everything from a new policy for food left in the fridge to an impending IRS audit. But no one expected what it was *really* about.

At 2:00 we all crowded into Conference B to hear the big announcement. Rustin was still nowhere to be seen. He hadn't been on campus all day. He just sent a mysterious email to everyone and then left us hanging. When he finally showed up at about 2:10, our levels of excitement and anxiety were at a fever pitch. He made his way to the front of the room and turned to address all of us.

"Thanks for meeting with me here today. I am sure that you all curious about the big announcement. Just to ease your mind, I want to let you know it's a good thing."

You could feel the sense of relief that went out through the office when he said that.

"We've been together for a number of years now, and it's been a great ride. Some of you have been here since the beginning," he said, looking at me. "And some of you just joined the team." He looked over at some of the guys working the call center. "It's been a great ride, but for me that ride is over."

Someone gasped. What was he saying? Where was he going with all of this?

"Guys, we've been bought out. I just finished a deal with Google. They love Helix and they bought the company. You'll all keep your jobs, but you'll be working for someone else from now on."

Now everyone was buzzing. Google! Wow. We've hit the big time. I immediately wondered how much Rustin got for the company. I'm guessing it was in the tens of millions. I had seen the sales numbers for the last few quarters—we were strong and getting stronger. I imagined Rustin was going to retire and move to some beach where he would wear his cutoffs and flip flops again. Wow. Talk about a payoff. But I couldn't imagine a better guy for that to happen to.

***

So that was it. Rustin was on the way out and the new ownership was on the way in. That was the last surprise he had for us. Or so we thought.

A few weeks later, we had an office party on the last day Rustin was to work before handing the company off to the new owners. It was a typical office party—we decorated the office multi-purpose room with streamers and a homemade banner that said "congratulations Rustin." Appropriately, we went with a tropical theme complete with rented tiki torches and a couple of surfboards in the corner.

We ate our cake, drank our punch, and we shared colorful anecdotes of things Rustin had done in the years we knew him. It was good closure. When we were done, Rustin made his way to the front of the room with a stack of envelopes in his hand. He looked out at us and he said:

"Guys, thanks for doing this for me. I had a great time working with all of you. You are the best team that I could have hoped for, and I think you are going to do even bigger and better things in the years ahead. This is just the beginning for you guys.

"Before I leave the office for the last time, I want to give you guys something as an expression of my thanks. I've said it before and I will say it again, Helix would not have happened without each and every one of you. This is your project, and you should be proud of yourselves. I want to show you how much I appreciate your hard work. So first, Melanie, would you come up here?"

The receptionist made her way to the front. She had been with the company for a few months, ever since the move to the downtown office, but Rustin had really taken a liking to her. When she got to the front of the room, Rustin handed her an envelope. She smiled as she accepted it.

"Open it," he said, beaming. The receptionist worked the envelope open and then pulled out a piece of paper that was obviously a check. But she had the strangest look on her face as she looked at the check, and then at Rustin, and then back to the check.

"This can't be right," she said. I didn't get it.

"No it's right," Rustin said. "Thanks for your hard work."

She looked up at the rest of us and then turned the check around to face us. "It's a check for three-point-two million dollars," she said.

People gasped. Mark from accounting choked on his cake. There were rumors that Rustin was sleeping with the receptionist, but you'd think he'd be a little more subtle about it. Wow. That girl just walked into a gold mine. People would be talking about this for years. Three-point-two million dollars? Had he lost his mind? If he wasn't careful he was going to blow through his retirement in a couple of months and he'd be back here looking for a job.

When the crowd got over the shock of seeing the new girl walk away with her big payoff, Rustin called the next name. "Howard, would you come up here?" Howard worked in the call center. He seemed like a nice guy, but I didn't know him too well since he only worked part time. Howard jumped out of his seat and made his way to the front. Just as before, Rustin handed him and envelope. Howard didn't waste any time. He tore open the envelope and his eyes got huge. He held the check high and shouted out, "Three-point-two million dollars!"

Mark started choking again. Maybe Rustin wasn't sleeping with the receptionist. Maybe he had lost his mind. Sometimes when people experience significant stress in their lives, they snap and lose their sense of rational behavior. Apparently this is what happened to Rustin.

Maybe I had vastly underestimated the value of the company and Rustin's bargaining skills. Was the deal worth hundreds of millions of dollars? How did he pull that off? As I was trying to work out a scenario in my head, I almost missed Mark from accounting getting his check for 3.2

million dollars. When he opened the envelope, he hugged Rustin so tight he grunted in pain, "Thanks Mark. You're welcome."

I don't know how he did it, but Rustin had worked out an outlandish deal with Google and now he was sharing the wealth. My mind immediately went to how much money I would make. If the receptionist made 3.2 million and the call-center guy made 3.2 million, my paycheck would have to be in the eight figures. After all, it was my program. I made Helix. It was my baby. I was the one that brought this fortune to Rustin. He owed me.

But what would I spend it on? I started thinking about which I'd prefer—beachfront property or something on the slopes? Regardless, I think the first order of business would be to upgrade my ride. I think a Ferrari would look good parked out in front of either option. I was so caught up in my fantasy that I almost missed Rustin giving a check for 3.2 million dollars to Bill, one of the programmers we hired after the *PC Magazine* article.

As Rustin made his way through the staff—the most recent hires first and the old-timers last, I settled on the beachfront property and a red Ferrari. I don't see how it could be any other way. But as I envisioned myself cruising the boardwalk in style, I heard Rustin say:

"Well, I have one more envelope left. This one goes out to the guy with the big idea." He looked at me. "Five or so years ago, I ran into Brian at a job fair. He was wearing a Family Guy T-shirt and he wasn't having any luck with the corporate stiffs. But he told me about this idea he had for an operating system he called Helix. He said it was going to change the world. And you know what, he was right. Everything that you see here in this office is a direct result of his ideas. Brian, thank you. None of this would have been possible without you."

As I made my way to the front of the room, my coworkers thundered with applause. People were whistling. Others were cheering. Some were chanting my name. "Bri-an! Bri-an!" I hugged Rustin and then accepted the envelope that he handed me. "Go ahead," he said, "Open it."

I fumbled with the envelope. I was trembling with excitement. Finally, I got it open and looked down at the check inside. My jaw dropped. My head started spinning. I felt ill. There staring back at me was a check for 3.2 million dollars.

This couldn't be real. He gave that much to the receptionist and the guy who worked part time. I had slaved away for him for five years. It was my idea. How could we receive the same amount? I looked up at Rustin in disbelief. I wanted to say something, but my mouth just hung open, speechless. I thought I was going to pass out.

Rustin was just standing there with a stupid grin on his face. He didn't get it. "You're welcome," he said, reaching out to hug me again. I dodged his arms and ran out of the room, head still spinning. All eyes were on me as I barreled out of the room and into the hallway.

When I got into the hallway, I had to brace myself against a wall to keep from falling over. Was this a dream? Was this really happening? How could Rustin do this to me after all I did for him? As I was trying to make sense of everything that happened, Rustin chased me out of the multi-purpose room.

"Are you okay?" he asked. "You look like you're going to puke."

"How? Why? I don't understand..." I stumbled for words as I tried to process what was happening to me.

Rustin smiled. "I wanted to share the wealth. You guys worked hard to make this happen and I wanted to give back."

I don't know if it was the self-righteous tone of his voice or the stupid grin on his face, but something about him made me snap. He obviously didn't get it. He had taken advantage of me and he thought he was doing a good deed.

"Give back?! Give back?! Is that what you call it? Melanie has been with the company for less than six months! And Howard? Howard answers phones! How could you give them the same as me?! I slaved for you for five years. All the ideas were mine. How is that fair?"

With that last accusation, I saw the joy leave Rustin's countenance. I could tell my words hurt him deeply. It felt strangely good.

Rustin looked down at the ground and then back up at me. I could tell he was searching for the right words to say. "You're right. It's not fair.... It's generous."

"What do you mean?" I asked indignantly.

"Brian, what was the deal we made when I hired you?"

My mind went back to that day at the fair. He had me there. "Well, that's not the point," I said.

"No, that *is* the point." He said. "What was the deal you made?"

"I agreed to make Helix for you." I said reluctantly.

"Right." Rustin said. "You agreed to make it for me. I took the risk. The product was developed on my dollar. I had everything to lose and everything to gain. And did I ever fail to pay you?"

"No." He had me there.

"And did I ever promise to give you *anything* beyond a paycheck?"

"No."

"And that check in your hands for 3.2 million dollars. Did you ever think you would make that much money?"

I had to admit, I never *did* think I would make that much money. Not in my wildest dreams. I was holding a check for more money than most people see in their whole lives. "No," I answered. "I never thought I would make this much money."

"How have I wronged you?"

His words hung in the air for what seemed like an eternity. How *had* he wronged me? He gave me more than I ever could have asked for. Than why was I so angry?

"Brian, what I decide to give to my other employees is between me and them. It is nothing of your concern. I gave you more than I ever promised you and you are set for life. If I want to take the money I made from this deal, split it twenty ways and give it back to the people I work with, that's my prerogative. Am I not allowed to do what I choose with what belongs to me? Or do you begrudge my generosity?"

Again, I was speechless. I just stood there dumbfounded looking at him. I could see the hurt in his eyes. He *had* been generous. He gave me more than I deserved. I stood there looking at him, and he turned and walked off toward the elevator.

I stood there in the hallway, check in hand, not knowing what to do. I had just scorned the man who had done more for me than anyone I had ever known. What was I going to do with that?

As I stood there trying to figure out what to do next, something Rustin said came back to my mind. He said he split the money he made twenty ways. But there were twenty-one employees if you counted Rustin himself. But who...? He gave everyone an envelope. But that would mean.... When I realized what he did, I raced off toward the elevator after him.

*"For the kingdom of heaven is like a master of a house who went
out early in the morning to hire laborers for his vineyard. After
agreeing with the laborers for a denarius a day, he sent them into
his vineyard. And going out about the third hour he saw others
standing idle in the marketplace, and to them he said, 'You go
into the vineyard too, and whatever is right I will give you.' So
they went. Going out again about the sixth hour and the ninth
hour, he did the same. And about the eleventh hour he went
out and found others standing. And he said to them, 'Why do
you stand here idle all day?' They said to him, 'Because no one
has hired us.' He said to them, 'You go into the vineyard too.'
And when evening came, the owner of the vineyard said to his
foreman, 'Call the laborers and pay them their wages, beginning with the last, up to the first.' And when those hired about
the eleventh hour came, each of them received a denarius. Now
when those hired first came, they thought they would receive
more, but each of them also received a denarius. And on receiv-
ing it they grumbled at the master of the house, saying, 'These
last worked only one hour, and you have made them equal to us
who have borne the burden of the day and the scorching heat.'
But he replied to one of them, 'Friend, I am doing you no wrong.
Did you not agree with me for a denarius? Take what belongs to
you and go. I choose to give to this last worker as I give to you.
Am I not allowed to do what I choose with what belongs to me?
Or do you begrudge my generosity?' So the last will be first, and
the first last." (Matthew 20:1–16)*

IN EPHESIANS 1, PAUL reminds us of all the blessings that are ours in Christ.
God chose us to be holy and blameless (v. 4). He adopted us as children (v.
5). He has redeemed us from slavery to sin and death (v. 6). He has given
us spiritual wisdom and understanding (vv. 8–9). He has chosen us as his
special people (v. 11), and he has promised us an inheritance (v. 14).

Paul goes on to say that these riches are not ours because we deserve them, but because God has blessed us in Christ. "It is by grace you have been saved through faith," he famously wrote.[1]

Christians have long celebrated this foundational truth: salvation is a gift from God that cannot be earned. And yet, we always seem to be on the lookout for things to earn.

When I was growing up, I was taught in Sunday school about "eternal rewards" in heaven. I think the idea came from 1 Corinthians 3:10–15. I was told that everything I did in life was either a good or worthless deed. Good deeds were stored up in heaven as precious stones or metals, and worthless deeds were stored up as wood, hay, and straw. At the end of time, God would burn up everyone's heavenly treasures, and whatever was left could be used to construct some kind of mansion in heaven.

This always bothered me.

I always imagined the guy who believed in Jesus but then still had problems. He didn't do a lot of good deeds in life and at the end most of his stuff was burned up, leaving little with which to construct his heavenly mansion.

What if that guy had to live next door to Mother Teresa for eternity?

Every day, he would come home from his heavenly vocation only to be reminded of all the ways he fell short in life. Conversely, Mother Teresa would be tempted to take great pride in her beautiful mansion that reminded the rest of her brothers and sisters in Christ how much better than them she was.

Something just seems wrong about that to me.

In Matthew 20, Jesus tells a parable about a guy who goes out early in the morning to look for laborers for his vineyard. He finds some, and settles on a fair price for a day's labor. Later, he goes back to the marketplace and finds some people who haven't found work yet. He hires them, too, and agrees to pay them what's appropriate. He does this again and again. Then, at the end of the day, he goes to settle accounts, starting with those hired last. Shockingly, he pays them exactly what those hired first agreed to work for. Then, working backward, he pays everyone the same.

Understandably, those hired first are indignant. They bore the brunt of the labor and the heat of the day—how was it fair that they be paid the same as those hired last? The owner's response is stunning: "You're right; it's not fair."

---

1. Ephesians 2:8.

Grace is *never* fair, and we don't want it to be.

Grace isn't unfair because it gives us *less* than we deserve; it's unfair because it gives us *more* than we deserve. Even those hired first get more than they deserve. Remember all the blessings Paul talked about in Ephesians 1? We don't deserve any of that. Why, then, are we so drawn to systems that emphasize fairness? Jesus asks us in his parable, "Do you begrudge my generosity?"[2]

Chilling words.

Jesus is generous with *all of us,* and if he chooses to be more generous with some than others, that is his prerogative.

Here's how I imagine what is going to happen in the end times. This isn't based on any specific Bible verses, it's just what my gut tells me based on my understanding of God's story. Take it or leave it. Perhaps we *do* get evaluated for every good and careless deed done in life. Maybe the good ones get stored away as precious stones or metals, and the careless ones end up as flammable materials. Then comes the great inferno that tests the value of everyone's works.

Here's where things get interesting—what if we get a choice?

If everyone goes through this process, that means Jesus himself goes through it. Jesus's hoard of precious gems and metals is going to be *immense.* After all, he led a sinless life and did countless righteous deeds.

So, what if the pile of precious materials based on *our works* becomes Pile A, and the pile based on *Jesus's* works becomes Pile B? Through faith in Christ, what is true of Jesus is true of us, so what if we get to *pick* the pile from which we want to build our heavenly mansion? We can build with our own works, or we can build with Jesus's works as if they were our own.

I know which one I am taking.

QUESTIONS FOR REFLECTION

1. Have you ever seen someone blessed for free with something that you had to work for? How did that feel?

2. How do you think the original hearers of this parable reacted? If you were in that audience, what would *you* have said to Jesus?

3. Read Ephesians 1:1–14. What blessing are you most grateful for?

---

2. Matthew 20:15.

4. Who are some kinds of people that we tend to think don't deserve the same heavenly reward we anticipate?

5. Why is it so hard for us to see others blessed with things they don't deserve?

6. What can we do to better cultivate a heart of gratitude—where we can rejoice with people when they receive blessings they don't deserve?

Court

"So now faith, hope, and love abide, these three; but the greatest of these is love." (1 Corinthians 13:13)

MAIA TOOK HER COMPACT mirror out of her purse for one last look as she stood in the hallway outside of the courtroom. She wasn't sure what she thought she might see, but the act itself was calming.

"You're going to do great," she heard Roger say beside her. She looked over at him and saw that her attorney was casually flipping through his phone. *I guess my life is interrupting him from more important things*, she thought.

Roger's lax attitude made her wonder if it was a mistake to hire him on the recommendation of a friend instead of doing the research herself.

"When are we going to go in?" her daughter said as she fidgeted, leaning against the wall.

"Be patient, Maisie," she scolded her eight-year-old. "This isn't fun for any of us."

"Especially not Dad," her twelve-year-old cut in. He didn't even take his nose out of his book to make the comment—he seemed bothered even to be there.

"You're not helping, Leland," she said to the boy. "And why don't you put that book down and be present with us for once," she added.

"This going to be easy," Roger interrupted. "Given your employment stability and Charlie's addictions, you are going to get full custody. It's just a matter of how much contact he can have with them."

"Well, considering what he has put us through, I want as much as I can get. He has no money, so time is what I want."

"Sure," Roger said, not looking up from his phone.

"When are we going to go in?!" Maisie moaned.

"Be patient!" Maia snapped at her daughter. "*Soon.*"

Roger looked up from his phone. "Are you sure you want this all on you?" He glanced over at the young girl who was growing more agitated. "It might be nice to have Charlie's help once in a while—you know, give you a break? It could be good for *them*, too."

Maia's brow furrowed. Good for *them*? She wasted seventeen years with Charlie. She should be farther in life than she was, and it was *his* fault. She wanted the judge to recognize that.

"I am sure," she said emphatically. "Charlie is a train wreck."

"What's a train wreck?" Maisie asked, hopping between the colored tiles on the hallway floor.

"It's a metaphor," Leland responded, still not taking his nose out of that blasted book. "She means that she doesn't want Dad to take care of us."

"Your father *can't* take care of you," Maia interrupted. "Leland, can you take Maisie for a walk? I am having a grown-up conversation right now."

Leland finally peeled his eyes off the book only to roll them as he reached for Maisie's hand. "Come on," he sighed.

Maia looked back at Roger. The attorney watched her children walking away with a frown on his face.

"They'll thank me when they're older," she said emphatically.

Roger shrugged. "Yeah. Have you thought about Charlie? Do you think this is the best for him?"

"Charlie?" Maia responded indignantly. "He made his bed. I am not worried about what is best for him."

"Right." Roger hesitated, choosing his words carefully. "Do you think his years of service affected him? I mean, he must have seen some stuff over there."

"Excuses," Maia said. "Look, combat changed him. I don't deny that. I know he has injuries. I get that. But opioids are *not* the answer. It's not an excuse, and I shouldn't have to suffer for *his* choices."

"All right," Roger said. "Look, Charlie's only hope is to remind the judge of his military service. Anything you can do to counteract that would help."

"What can I do?" Maia asked. She was starting to get eager for a fight.

Well," Roger said. "We got Judge Mancilla. He's a good family man and very religious." A lightbulb seemed to go on in Roger's mind. "Are you religious?" he asked.

"Religious?" Maia scoffed. "No."

Roger frowned again. "You don't have any stories of going to church or anything you could tell?"

Maia thought. "Not since I was a kid," she finally said. "It's not really my thing."

Roger nodded and returned to his thoughts.

"Oh!" Maia said. "My friend Celeste is always inviting me to *her* church. I can tell him that I am going with her."

Roger smiled. "I think that would help."

Just then the doors opened, and the court was ready for them to enter.

Maia made her way to the front of the court and sat down with Roger. Her kids took up the row behind them as they waited for the judge.

A few minutes later, Charlie arrived, disheveled and late—as always. He grimaced in pain as he shuffled his way to the front and sat down opposite Maia.

Moments later, everyone rose as the judge came in. They were seated and he began to comment.

"I have been looking over your case," the judge began, "Mr. Holmes, I am concerned for you. Your lack of employment, your drug habit, and your living conditions do not seem promising for raising children. Don't you agree?"

Charlie did not look up at the judge but spoke into a mic at the table. "Yes, Your Honor."

"What lessons would your lifestyle teach your children?" the judge continued. "Maisie is only eight. Can you keep her safe?"

"Probably not," Charlie said. He was struggling to keep his composure.

"You son is twelve. What lessons would he learn from you?"

"Not good ones," Charlie said.

The judge turned to face Maia. "Ms. Holmes, your growth has been impressive. It seems like you have built quite a life for yourself. Can you elaborate a bit about what it is that you do?"

"I am a health and fitness influencer, Your Honor. I use social media and the internet to help people stay healthy and fit—recipes, exercise routines, things like that."

The judge nodded as she explained. "I am looking at your tax records," he said. "All of that income comes from your internet business?"

"Yes, Your Honor," Maia said.

The judge's eyes brightened. "Very impressive. You should be proud of yourself."

A slight smile began to stretch across Maia's face. "Well, God has been good to me." She noticed the judge's eyes brighten again.

"I *can't wait* for church this Sunday," she added.

The judge smiled, but his smile faded as he turned to Charlie. "Mr. Holmes, I am saddened and disappointed in your case. Thank you for your service, but I cannot in good conscience entrust you with children until you get your life together. If you want to be in your kids' lives, you need to get clean. You need to get a job. And you need to get a stable living condition."

"Yes, your honor," Charlie said, choking back tears. He still didn't look up.

Charlie shuffled out of the courtroom, grimacing with his head held low. He knew the judge was right. He knew his kids were better off with their mother. He knew he needed to get it together. He had barely taken two steps into the hallway before he was grabbed from behind and almost tackled by small arms. Pain shot up his back and he tried not to scream.

"Daddy!" Maisie shouted from behind him.

"Sweetheart!" he said, turning around and forcing a smile.

"When are we going to see you again?" Maisie asked. Charlie noticed Maia and Leland following her out of the courtroom. Maia was scowling.

"Well, we'll have to talk to Mom about that," he said.

Maia looked over at Leland. "Leland, can you take Maisie for another walk?"

When the kids were gone, Maia turned her gaze to Charlie with fire in her eyes. "You brought this on yourself, Charlie. *I* am the one raising them while *you* just garner sympathy. *I* built a business that paid the bills. *I* took them to school. *I* went to the PTA meetings. They even made me the head of the PTA!"

"You're right," Charlie said. "They are better off with you. But they still need me in their life."

"They're kids," Maia insisted. "They don't know *what* they need. They'll thank me when they're older. You heard the judge—*you* need to get your life together."

Charlie looked at the floor and nodded.

"I tell you what," Maia said. "I am going to church with my friend Celeste on Sunday. Maybe you can take the kids out to lunch afterward."

"You're going to church?" Charlie asked in disbelief.

"I know; it's dumb." Maia admitted. "But there's a lot of potential clients at that church."

"Clients?" Charlie asked.

"*One of us* has to pay the bills," she said.

"All right," Charlie said. "See you Sunday."

Maia stormed off and got the kids. Charlie waved as they left.

Church, Charlie thought. He couldn't imagine Maia at a church. But thinking about church spurred a longing inside of him.

Maybe *he* could go to church. Charlie thought he remembered seeing an old church on the way to the courthouse. It was even in walking distance. Maybe he could go there. Maybe they would be open.

He left the courthouse and walked the two blocks to the church. Old, gray bricks and stained glass framed an imposing wooden door of the church. He tried the door—it opened.

Charlie made his way into the church foyer and looked around the dimly lit room. Old paintings of Jesus and other biblical scenes covered the walls of the foyer, and chairs and potted plants peppered the space. He looked around, trying to figure out what to do next.

A voice echoed from down the hall. "Hello?"

Charlie turned to see an elderly priest enter the foyer. His thick glasses and wispy white hair betrayed decades in the ministry.

"Oh, hi." Charlie responded. "Are you open? I don't really know what for; I'm not really a church person, but I thought I might stop in for a few minutes and collect my thoughts."

"Well, I am the only one here right now," the priest said, but you are welcome to have a seat in the sanctuary if you want some time to pray."

Pray? thought Charlie. He wasn't even sure he knew how to do that. "Thank you," was all he thought to say.

"I'm Father Giroux," the priest said, extending his hand. "Let me show you to the sanctuary."

The priest led the way and, after Charlie took a seat in one of the back-row pews, he turned to leave. "My study is just down the hall if you need anything," he said. "If not, just close the door when you leave." At that, Father Giroux departed, leaving Charlie alone in the sanctuary, lit only by the sunlight coming through the stained glass.

Charlie looked around. Being here was like entering a time warp—the stained glass, the strange artwork, the wooden pews. Charlie saw a crucifix on one of the walls. It was a strange sight to Charlie. He had seen crucifixes many times before and never given them a second look, but this time he did look and what he saw fascinated him.

Jesus was gaunt—his cheeks sunken. His eyes wild with a look of both pain and determination. A crown of thorns sat on his head and blood trickled down his face.

At first, Charlie recoiled. Such a strange thing for a church to celebrate. And yet, he couldn't look away. As disturbing as the depiction of Jesus was, it was also intriguing and somewhat beautiful to think of God this way—twisted in pain and sorrow.

Charlie didn't know what to pray. He didn't know *how* to pray. So, he sat there, gazing at Jesus in silence.

He sat there for an hour, reflecting on his life, reflecting on God, when the priest finally returned.

"You're still here?" he said with some disbelief. "I am sorry I didn't check in earlier. I assumed you had left."

"That's okay," Charlies said. "I am not part of your flock. Should I leave now?"

The old priest chuckled. "No, you don't have to leave. Do you mind if I ask whether you found the answers you were looking for?"

Charlie smiled awkwardly and looked at the ground. "I am not exactly sure what I came here for," he said. "I guess I was hoping God would speak to me."

"Well, God can speak to you anywhere. He can certainly speak to you here. What are you hoping he will say?"

Tears began to form in Charlie's eyes. "I have made a lot of mistakes in my life. I've done things I am not proud of. I've hurt people. I've tried to change, but I can't. I am afraid that I have lost my kids forever."

"I see," the priest responded. "I am so sorry to hear that. You know, God knows what it is like to lose a son."

Charlie looked up at the priest puzzled. Then, it hit him. "Oh. You mean like the whole Jesus the Son of God thing?"

"Exactly."

Charlie nodded in thought. "What's the deal with you Christians and Jesus, anyway? I have been sitting here for an hour looking at that statue up there. He looks so broken and defeated. It bothers me."

"It bothers me, too," the priest said, looking up at the crucifix. "And yet, I can't look away."

"Yes. Exactly!" Charlie said.

"That is the beauty of the cross," the priest began. "On the cross, God himself bore our sins. He took our pain. Our wounds. Our mistakes. Our wrongdoing. He bore them on himself so that *we* might be healed."

"I don't understand."

"Well," Father Giroux continued, "It's sort of mystical. When God became human, he united himself to us and our fate became tied to his. Think of when you got married—before you were married you were your own person, and your wife was her own person. When you married, you united and became something new."

"OK," Charlie said. "So, Jesus is like a God-Man hybrid?"

"Not a hybrid," Giroux said. "Fully God, fully human, without the mixing of the two. It's complicated."

"Yeah."

"You see," the priest continued, "Jesus was perfect and holy, but as you can see from our artwork—he suffered. He suffered unjustly and died for the sins of humanity. Remember the mystical union? As God and man, he could suffer for you and me."

"So, when you look at Jesus, you see yourself?" Charlie asked.

"Exactly," the priest said. "But that's not all I see, because Jesus' story did not end on the cross. Three days later, he rose from the dead, signifying victory over sin and death. So, when I look at that image of Jesus, not only do I see my sins, but I am also reminded that I am united to Christ in his resurrection. My sin will not get the last laugh. Death is not the end."

Tears again began to form in Charlie's eyes. "That is a good thought," he said. "I can see how you find that beautiful." Charlie again looked at the image of Jesus. "It is a strangely compelling message. I envy you. I wish I could have the hope you have. Sadly, I am too far gone. There is nothing God could do with someone like me."

"Look again," Giroux responded.

Charlie again looked at the broken body of Jesus impaled on the cross. Somehow, his protruding ribs and battered face reminded him of himself. Maybe not on the outside, but on the *inside*.

The priest said, "There are no limits to Jesus's mercy. He didn't come for the righteous, but for sinners. That means you, my friend."

Charlie wanted to believe that.

***

That Sunday, Maia waited for Charlie outside a large evangelical church with her friend, Celeste. He was late, again.

"Thanks for inviting us to your church," Maia said to her friend. "I hadn't been since I was a kid. It's a lot different than I remember."

"Oh of course," Celeste said cheerfully. "You're always welcome. I'm here every Sunday."

Just then another woman bounded by on her way to her car. She tapped Maia's shoulder as she passed and held out a small card in her other hand. "Nice to meet you today, Maia. I will be in touch!" she called as she scurried off, waving what Celeste realized was a business card. The woman had a spring in her step, but her floral pattern dress had no form to it and her hair looked unkempt.

"She needs more help than I can give, am I right?" Maia said to Celeste under her breath.

Celeste's jaw dropped. "She's nice," she said. "You should have coffee with her. I think you would like her."

Maia looked at her like she was from another planet. "You're hilarious. I don't think I could be friends with her. But she could make a good client."

Celeste countenance dropped a little. "How many of those cards did you give out today?"

"Like twenty," Maia responded. "I can't believe I didn't think of this before—there are a lot of potential clients at church. Plus, I think I can work it into my brand to help me stand out. I could be like a *Christian* health and fitness influencer."

"Well, it could also be good for you and your family to be here," Celeste said. "You've been through a lot lately—I am sure you have a lot on your mind."

"Seriously," Maia said. "But, after seventeen years with Charlie, I am used to it. Some people are just hopeless. You do everything you can to help them, and it doesn't matter. I am so glad I am not one of those people. Look at me. I was fully dependent on him, but I started my own business, I've grown it to where I can support myself, I got the kids through school, I was even made president of the PTA. I'm not one of those people who just makes excuses or gives up. You have to rise above."

"Yeah, I guess," Celeste said reluctantly. "We all have our problems, though. Charlie has seen a lot in life—who knows what we would do if we were in his situation."

"Don't let him fool you," Maia said. As she was about to continue, a car pulled into the church parking lot. "Oh, speak of the devil."

Charlie pulled up next to Maia and the kids and rolled down the window. "Sorry I am late," he said.

"Hi, Dad!" the two kids screamed simultaneously.

A huge smile spread over their dad's face. "Hi, kids!" he said. "Are you hungry?"

"Yes!" Maisie said excitedly as each kid grabbed a door handle and got in the car.

Charlie looked up at Maia. "What time should I bring them back here?"

"Two o'clock," Maia said. "Celeste and I are getting lunch and then we'll meet back here."

"Dad, what's that?" Maisie's voice called from inside the car. She was pointing at a crucifix hanging from the read-view mirror of his car.

Charlie looked embarrassed. "Oh, that's just something I got at church."

"You went to church?" asked Maisie, her eyes brightening.

"Well, yeah. I went the other day to talk to someone."

"That's good." Maia rolled her eyes. "Maybe they can help you get your life together."

Charlie turned his look from Maisie to Maia. "Yeah, I was surprised. It was beautiful to pray there. I am going back next week."

"Oh! Can we go with dad next week?" Leland said from inside the car.

Maia stooped to speak to her son in the back seat. "No, you're going to come to this church with me next week."

"Aaaaaaaaah. I wanna go with Daddy," Maisie said.

Maia looked at Charlie with fire in her eyes.

"I- I could pick them up next week—"

"Can you be on time?" Maia snapped.

"Yes. Eight thirty. I'll be there."

"Yeah!" both kids screamed from the back seat.

Maia sighed and shook her head as Charlie rolled up the window and drove the kids off to lunch.

"Kids," Maia said, disgusted. "They have *no idea* what is good for them. Do you see what I have to put up with?"

Celeste didn't answer, but instead asked, "Does that mean you'll come by yourself next week?"

Maia glanced down at the stack of business cards in her hand and her eyes lit up. "Of course!" she said. "Can you tell me more about what the Bible says about health? Doesn't it say something about our bodies being a temple? I think I could use that for my branding. I am *so glad* I decided to come here today."

68

"He also told this parable to some who trusted in themselves that they were righteous, and treated others with contempt: 'Two men went up into the temple to pray, one a Pharisee and the other a tax collector. The Pharisee, standing by himself, prayed thus: "God, I thank you that I am not like other men, extortioners, unjust, adulterers, or even like this tax collector. I fast twice a week; I give tithes of all that I get." But the tax collector, standing far off, would not even lift up his eyes to heaven, but beat his breast, saying, "God, be merciful to me, a sinner!" I tell you, this man went down to his house justified, rather than the other. For everyone who exalts himself will be humbled, but the one who humbles himself will be exalted.'" (Luke 18:9–14)

IN MARK 12, THERE is a story about a bunch of teachers of the law debating with Jesus, asking him questions, and trying to catch him in his words. In the midst of the debate, one teacher asks Jesus a genuine question: Which commandment is the most important? Jesus famously answers that the most important is to love the Lord with all your heart, soul, mind, and strength, and the second is this: Love your neighbor as yourself. Paul echoed Jesus's teaching: "For the whole law is fulfilled in one word: 'You shall love your neighbor as yourself.'"[1]

There are *a lot* of commands in the Bible—and not just in the Old Testament. Jesus said: "Do not lay up for yourselves treasures on earth."[2]

Paul said: "Flee from sexual immorality."[3]

James said: "Submit yourselves therefore to God."[4]

These commands in the Bible are not just bonus material for those who want to enjoy the special collector's edition—they are *part* of it. Christianity is not just a belief system; it is a way of life.

Through the commands, the Scriptures paint a picture of the life that is truly living. Moses said to Israel about the Law: "I have set before you

1. Galatians 5:14.
2. Matthew 6:19.
3. 1 Corinthians 6:18.
4. James 4:7.

life and death, blessing and curse. Therefore choose life, that you and your offspring may live."[5]

Jesus said about his teaching: "For the gate is narrow and the way is hard that leads to life, and those who find it are few."[6]

Paul, the champion of grace, said: "For if you live according to the flesh you will die, but if by the Spirit you put to death the deeds of the body, you will live."[7]

The Scriptures portray a way of life that is truly living, and that way of life can be summarized in the two greatest commandments: Love God and love others.

In Luke 18, Jesus tells this story about a guy who misses the forest for the trees. He is so concerned about the minutiae of the commandments that he forgets the heart: Love God and love others.

In Jesus's parable, two guys who go to the temple to pray. One is a Pharisee and one is a tax collector. The Pharisee prays mostly about himself: "Thank you God that I am awesome and not a loser like this tax collector." The tax collector, on the other hand, does not offer much of a prayer. He seems nervous even to *approach* God. He doesn't look up. He simply beats and breast and asks for mercy.

In Jesus's day, the Pharisees were respected—they were the upstanding citizens of Judea (like social media influencers, entrepreneurs, and heads of the PTA). Tax collectors, on the other hand, were considered scoundrels (much like people today look down on those who have lost jobs and families due to addictions). The tax collector in this story is Jewish, but he works for Rome. He would have been considered by his countrymen a rascal and a traitor.

The original hearers of the story would have *expected* the Pharisee to be the hero. When he begins reciting a laundry list of his achievements, they would have been *even more* impressed. The tax collector is humble. He recognizes his own brokenness. But he's still a tax collector.

The shock of the story comes at the end, when Jesus says that the tax collector and not the Pharisee left there right in God's eyes.

Luke tells us the main point of the parable before it even begins: "He also told this parable to some who trusted in themselves that they were

---

5. Deuteronomy 30:19.

6. Matthew 7:14.

7. Romans 8:13.

righteous, and treated others with contempt."[8] In other words, there is a danger to being so impressed with your own virtue that you start to look down on others.

Whether you are as scandalous as a tax collector (or addict), or as polished as a Pharisee (or PTA president), your hope is the same—the mercy of God and the cross of Christ. The Scriptures tell us that *all* have sinned and fall short of the glory of God.[9] While Jesus shows us a way of life that is truly living, we will always fall short. Our hope is always Jesus—his death for sins and his resurrection.

The Pharisee's problem was not that he tithed and fasted.[10] Those were both good things. The Pharisee's problem was that he *trusted* in his own tithing and fasting, and consequently he treated people like the tax collector with contempt.

It is not a sin to want to live a virtuous life.

It *is* a sin to show others contempt.

We are often more like the tax collector than we realize. We greatly underestimate our own sinfulness. As a result, we greatly underestimate the grace of God and the love that he has for us in Jesus Christ. Jesus reminded us that it is not healthy people who need physicians, but the sick. He came to call *sinners*.[11]

We come to God's great banquet table not as the healthy but as the sick. And we find in the broken body and the spilled blood of Jesus, the grace that makes us well.

QUESTIONS FOR REFLECTION

1. Have you ever been made to feel guilty or not good enough? What was that like?

2. How do you think the crowd reacted when Jesus ended by saying the tax collector went home justified?

---

8. Luke 18:9.

9. Romans 3:23.

10. In Matthew 23:23, Jesus tells the Pharisees that their problem was not that they tithed, but that they neglected the weightier matters of the law.

11. Mark 2:17.

3. What do you think the two men in Jesus's parable were like? What did they look like? How did they act? If you were to hang out with them separately at a party, how would each of those conversations go?

4. What are some things that people today tend to take spiritual pride in or trust in today?

5. Who are some people we tend to look down on or show contempt for today?

6. How can we keep the perspective of the tax collector and not become like the Pharisee?

Brother

"Therefore I command you, 'You shall open wide your hand to your brother, to the needy and to the poor, in your land.'"
(Deuteronomy 15:11)

John finished his presentation on the water tower to unenthusiastic applause. He could tell it did not go as well as he had hoped. The locals in the crowd were talking among themselves in Quechua, but he couldn't understand or speak it.

The crowd's body language told him all he needed to know—the way they shifted in the folding chairs set up in the dirt field, their furrowed brows exaggerating the lines in their faces already weathered by high-altitude winds. He didn't see a sparkle in anyone's eyes—a sign that they had favorably caught his vision for a tower that would bring clean water to the impoverished neighborhood.

John felt the sudden desire to be back at the downtown resort where he was staying—or better still, back in his posh Los Angeles home. He felt good about himself roughing it out here in the slums, but he could only take it for so long before he needed to get back to civilization.

"That was good," his translator said to him in English.

"Do you think so?" John asked. "I can't tell what they're saying."

"Well, I think it might take time for them to appreciate the project," the translator said hesitantly. "I think they are processing."

"Processing," John echoed. "I hope they understand all the health benefits the tower will bring them. I wish PJ were here to present—this was always his part. He was better than me."

John's brother, Peter Bell, Jr. (or PJ, as everyone called him), had passed away tragically six months previously. He was only thirty-five. The two brothers had devoted the ten years after PJ's baseball career was cut short to humanitarian work—using John's engineering skills and PJ's business savvy to help a community in Bolivia overcome the health and sanitation challenges related to poverty. This water tower was the capstone project—PJ's life dream.

"Your brother is missed," the translator said.

"Yeah," John said. "I don't know what he enjoyed more, baseball or helping people." A smile crept over his face. "I am just glad I got to be a part of his life."

As John talked to his interpreter, a group of community leaders had formed in front of the crowd. They signaled to the translator that they had something to say to John.

The leader of the three spoke first—a heavyset man in his fifties with big hands and a bigger smile. He spoke in Quechua and the translator nodded, asking him questions every now and then. When the man was finished, the translator turned to John.

"So, he says that they are grateful for the money invested in their community, but they are requesting it be spent on something else. While the water tower would be nice, what they *really* want is a community center."

"A community center?" John asked, shocked. "I don't understand. They want *that* more than clean water?"

"Right. I asked about that. He says that coming together today reminded them of the importance of community. A couple of neighbors were able to settle a dispute during a break in the meeting, and others were able to meet newcomers and help them find resources. They neighborhood doesn't really have a good place where they can gather to help each other."

"That doesn't make sense," John said. "Tell them that the water tower will prevent *diseases*."

The translator nodded and began to speak to the leaders in Quechua. This time, it was one of the other leaders—a stern-looking woman holding a toddler at her hip—who spoke up. She argued passionately, her whole body animated with every word as she made the case for something John couldn't understand. The translator nodded as she spoke and then turned to John.

"She says that the water filters they have work just fine. She is grateful for all the education you have done on sanitation. Using the filters has helped her keep her kids safe. But she is alone—her husband is in Europe working. Sometimes she needs help with her house or with the kids and she doesn't know who to ask. She wishes there were a community center where the neighbors could all get together and talk about how they can help each other."

John didn't know what to say. He just stood there, confused. This water tower project was PJ's life dream. He needed to do this for his brother. The community leaders could pick up on John's indecision and all began to speak to the translator at once. The voices all talking over each other in a language he didn't speak overwhelmed John and he held his hands up in protest.

"Please," he said to the translator. "Can you ask them to think about it for three days. Tell them I will reach out to them specifically to talk about this again."

The translator relayed the message. The leaders tried to smile and nod their heads, but John could tell they were dismayed.

John packed up his supplies and began to head back to his rental car when he heard someone behind him address him in English.

"Hey, brother," he called. "Can I talk to you for a moment?"

John turned to see a man in his thirties wearing a baseball cap, slacks, and a collared shirt rushing up to him. His dress seemed out of place in the area.

"Hi," John said. "Yes, I have a minute."

"My name is Pedro," the man said. "I was sitting in on your presentation."

"Oh." John shook his hand. "Thanks for coming out."

Pedro winced as they shook hands. "Sorry," Pedro said, pulling back his hand and grabbing his elbow. "Old elbow injury."

"No, *I* am sorry." John insisted. "I shouldn't have shaken so hard. I know how painful elbow injuries can be—my brother PJ threw out his UCL playing baseball. Ended his career. That's what brought us out here."

"Oh," Pedro said. "I know you two were close. Anyway, I can tell you put a lot of thought into this water tower project, but have you considered using the money to build a community center instead?"

John's shoulder slumped. He wished PJ had been here to do the presentation—he was so much more captivating of a speaker. Now the whole project was at risk.

"Well, we're talking about it. That's just not what our vision was."

"I know, brother," Pedro said apologetically. "But I think it is the vision of the people. I think you should listen to them. They have good reasons for wanting a community center."

John frowned. "I'm giving a lot of money for this project. I am starting to feel unappreciated. A water tower would change this community. Why don't they see that?"

Pedro saddened. "They do. And they are grateful, brother. They just want you to listen to them and consider their views."

"All right," was all John could say. "It was nice to meet you, Pedro. Have a good day."

John loaded the rental and drove back to the resort.

***

When John got back to the resort, he unloaded his gear and began thinking of his next move. *What am I going to do, PJ?* he thought. He wished his brother were there—he'd have a plan.

He needed something to clear his head—a shower, a good meal at the resort restaurant, a high-end whiskey, and maybe even a massage—that would help him think clearly.

He headed to the shower when he noticed something on the bedside table—a Bible.

It wasn't odd for a resort to have a Bible, but he didn't remember taking it out of the drawer or setting it on the bedside table.

Why would housekeeping get out a Bible?

Had someone else been in his room?

He went over to get a closer look and noticed something sticking out of it—a makeshift bookmark.

He opened the Bible and saw what was keeping the place—it was one of his brother's old baseball cards.

Peter Bell, Jr. Pitcher for Kansas City. Marked in the Bible in the place where it opened was Deuteronomy 15:11.

He read the verse:

"For there will never cease to be poor in the land. Therefore I command you, 'You shall open wide your hand to your brother, to the needy and to the poor, in your land.'" (Deut. 15:11)

The word "brother" was highlighted.

"Weird," John thought. "Where did this Bible come from and how did this baseball card get in it?" John usually kept the card in his wallet to remember PJ. He took his wallet out and checked—sure enough, the card was missing.

I must have dropped it, he thought. *Housekeeping must have found it and tucked it into this Bible.*

Still, it was kind of weird that a baseball card of his brother was tucked into a passage calling *the poor* his brother.

He shrugged off the coincidence and headed for the shower.

***

Four days later, John was at a luncheon at the resort's restaurant. The community leaders had been bused in from outside the city to hear one last pitch for a water tower in their neighborhood.

The meal was served, and about halfway through his food, John decided to get to work. The steak was a little overdone anyway, and the mashed potatoes were a little bland. He would get something else later.

"Thank you for joining me this afternoon," he began, and then waited for the translator.

"I'll never forget the day my brother found out he would never play ball again," he said, pausing after every sentence for translation. "He told me that he wanted the rest of his life to mean something. He wanted to help people—people like you—and he asked me if I wanted to join him. Since then, we have done great work in your community and your lives are better for it."

John looked out over the audience. He couldn't understand why, but the leaders weren't tracking with him. They seemed uncomfortable in the resort. Some of them had barely touched their food, as if they had been served diamonds on a plate of gold. They looked at him meekly as he continued the story of all the great work that he and PJ had done in the community.

"Sadly," John began his conclusion, "My brother never got to see the capstone of his vision—a water tower. But I am here to today to help bring that vision to fruition."

When he finished, the leaders looked at each other awkwardly. Finally, the heavyset man from the first meeting spoke up. When he had finished, the interpreter said to John, "He wonders if the vision could be accomplished with a community center."

John's heart sank. Not this again. He was starting to get frustrated. "I think you need a water tower."

The interpreter bit his lip and then relayed the message to the community leaders. This time, the woman who had the toddler at her hip earlier in the week spoke up.

"She says they have the filters," the interpreter began.

"*I know they have the filters!*" shouted John. He immediately regretted it.

The room was silent for a few moments before the interpreter began to relay the message.

"You don't have to tell them that," John said. "Look, this tower meant the world to my brother. It will save lives. I have worked hard raising money to build it—if there is no tower, there is no project."

Again there was silence.

"Do you want me to tell them that?" the interpreter asked.

"Yes," John said.

The interpreter explained the situation to the leaders and John saw the disappointment in their eyes. They talked to each other for a few moments and then the heavyset man said something to the interpreter as the group began to leave.

"They thank you for lunch and for helping their community."

John thanked them and sought the waiter to pay for the luncheon. *Where was that waiter*, he thought. *I barely saw him the whole lunch.*

On his way back to his car, John heard a familiar voice from behind him. "Brother, do you have a minute?"

John turned to see the young man in slacks and ball cap from the meeting the other day. John struggled to remember the man's name.

"Pedro," the man said with a smile.

That's right, Pedro. John thought. "I didn't see you in there," said with a smile. "I must have missed you."

"Oh yeah," Pedro responded. "Did you give any thought to what I said to you the other day?"

"What, about listening?" John asked.

"Yes," Pedro responded. "About treating them as brothers and sisters."

"What do you mean?" John asked again.

"Well, you come in here with all these ideas about how things should be. You have all these plans for how to make people's lives better. But you never stopped to ask what *they* wanted. When they worked up to courage to tell you what they wanted, you didn't listen."

"Well," John said. "There is a reason I am where I am, and they are where they are. Maybe I *do* know better."

"No, no, no, brother," Pedro began, shaking his head. "You can't think like that. You have been blessed. You enjoy luxuries like this resort every day, and most of them will never eat like this again. But the poor are our brothers and sisters."

John remembered the Bible verse—Deuteronomy something.

"Well, if they are," John spoke up, "They aren't *grateful* brothers and sisters. PJ spent his short life out here. All he wanted was to see a water tower built, and they can't even appreciate that."

"Your brother made mistakes," Pedro said meekly. Tears formed in his eyes. "Don't make the same mistakes."

"How do you know about my brother's mistakes?" John asked indignantly.

"I just know, brother," was all Pedro could say. "Listen, I have to go now. But I have one last word for you. The poor have a special place in God's heart, and he will defend them—in *this* life or the next."

At that, Pedro turned a walked away. John never saw him again.

***

Six months later, John presided over a ceremony to dedicate the new water tower. Turnout was less than he had expected. Empty chairs littered about and only a few people beyond the community leaders attended. *Well, they'll enjoy the water*, John thought.

He thanked the leaders for attending and helping make the project happen, gave a short speech about his brother and his dream for the tower, and then cut the ribbon to sparse applause. John felt like he was the only one smiling.

When it was over, the leaders approached him one last time. The looked defeated; their smiles forced. The woman spoke first.

"Thank you for the water tower," the translator clarified.

"You're very welcome," John said with a grin.

The heavyset man made a solemn comment and John looked over to the translator. "The poor have a special place in God's heart," the translator said.

John smiled. "Tell him he sounds like Pedro."

The translator relayed the message and the leaders looked confused. "They don't know who you're talking about," the translator said.

Now John was confused. "You know, Pedro. The guy with the slacks and the ballcap, injured elbow, calls people 'brother.' He was at all the meetings."

The translator relayed his message, and the leaders looked at each other, shaking their heads in confusion. The woman spoke and the translator said, "She says there was no one with that name at the meetings."

The heavyset man made a comment and the others all laughed in unison.

"What did he say?" John asked.

The translator was laughing, too. "He said, 'Maybe you saw a ghost!'" and they all laughed harder.

A ghost? John thought. Suddenly he noticed that there was something in his pocket. He reached in and pulled out the card—Peter Bell, Jr., pitcher for Kansas City. He noticed something else written on the card: "Don't make the same mistakes."

As he gazed at the card, he heard the leaders speak up once more as they walked away.

"Thanks again for the water tower," the translator said.

John's eyes went back to the card. "How do you know about my brother's mistakes?" He had asked Pedro.

"I just know, brother."

"There was a rich man who was clothed in purple and fine linen and who feasted sumptuously every day. And at his gate was laid a poor man named Lazarus, covered with sores, who desired to be fed with what fell from the rich man's table. Moreover, even the dogs came and licked his sores. The poor man died and was carried by the angels to Abraham's side. The rich man also died and was buried, and in Hades, being in torment, he lifted up his eyes and saw Abraham far off and Lazarus at his side. And he called out, 'Father Abraham, have mercy on me, and send Lazarus to dip the end of his finger in water and cool my tongue, for I am in anguish in this flame.' But Abraham said, 'Child, remember that you in your lifetime received your good things, and Lazarus in like manner bad things; but now he is comforted here, and you are in anguish. And besides all this, between us and you a great chasm has been fixed, in order that those who would pass from here to you may not be able, and none may cross from there to us.' And he said, 'Then I beg you, father, to send him to my father's house— for I have five brothers—so that he may warn them, lest they also come into this place of torment.' But Abraham said, 'They have Moses and the Prophets; let them hear them.' And he said, 'No, father Abraham, but if someone goes to them from the dead, they will repent.' He said to him, 'If they do not hear Moses and the Prophets, neither will they be convinced if someone should rise from the dead.'" (Luke 16:19–31)

IN THE BOOK OF Philemon, Paul writes to an ancient slaveowner by the name of Philemon on behalf of a runaway slave named Onesimus. The details of the situation aren't crystal clear, but it seems as if Onesimus ran away from Philemon and stole some things from him on the way out. When he was on the run, Onesimus met Paul, became a Christian, and even ministered to Paul in *his* imprisonment. Eventually, Paul challenged Onesimus to return home to Philemon, and he wrote the letter (now a book of the Bible) to accompany him.

In Philemon, Paul advocates hard for his new friend. He acknowledges Onesimus' wrongdoing and promises to pay Philemon back for any damages. At the same time, he encourages Philemon to forgive Onesimus as a personal favor to Paul. Having challenged Onesimus to return, Paul also challenges Philemon: "For this perhaps is why he was parted from you for a while, that you might have him back forever, no longer as a bondservant but more than a bondservant, as a beloved brother."[1]

Paul challenged Philemon to reimagine his relationship with Onesimus. No longer would they be master and bondservant—instead they would be brothers. This challenge permeates the New Testament. The early church considered themselves to be brothers and sisters worthy of compassion and familial loyalty.

In Luke 16, Jesus tells perhaps his strangest parable: The rich man and Lazarus. It's odd for a couple reasons. First, it is the only parable in which any of the characters are named—Abraham and Lazarus. Second, it takes place in hell (well, Hades anyway).

In the story, there is a poor man named Lazarus. And every day, Lazarus hangs out at the doorstep of a rich man and eats from his table scraps. In ancient dining, if you got sauce on your face, you would often wipe it with a piece of bread and throw it on the ground. That's probably what Lazarus was eating. Pretty gross.

Not only that, but Lazarus must have been sick, because he had open sores that the dogs licked every day. The ancient Israelites didn't keep dogs as pets, so these would have been wild street dogs, generally considered unclean and gross.

Lazarus had a pretty rough life.

But he dies and goes to what is called Abraham's bosom. The rich man dies as well and goes to Hades, where *he* is in torment.

The rich man sees Lazarus chilling with Abraham and he says, "Hey Abraham! Why don't you send Lazarus to bring me some water?"

Abraham says, "No; that can't happen. You had your share of good things in life. Now you're in torment. Lazarus is here with me and he's staying here."

So then, the rich man says, "Well, if you can't send Lazarus to help me, send him back to warn my brothers. I have five brothers—send him to them so they don't end up here with me."

1. Philemon 15–16.

Abraham says, "No. They have Moses and the prophets. They should listen to them. Otherwise, they wouldn't listen even if someone came back from the dead."

It's a strange story, and the key to understanding it is asking: Why is the rich man in hell (Hades, technically)?

Our first thought might be that the rich man is in hell because he is rich. But, Abraham was rich, too, and *he's* not in hell. So, it's not because he was rich.

Our second thought might be because he was rich and he didn't help Lazarus. I have heard Leonard Sweet teach on this and I love what he points out: Lazarus could have gone anywhere in town for help, but he *chose* to go to the rich man's house. Why?

He probably chose to go to the rich man's house because it's where he got the most or the best help. Think about it—who's going to have the nicest leftovers to give you? Rich people.

That raises the question, then, if the rich man is not in hell for being rich and he is not in hell because he didn't help the poor, why is he in hell?

Sweet says we get our answer in verse 28. In Jesus' story, the rich man says: "I have five brothers—[send Lazarus to them] so that he may warn them, lest they also come into this place of torment."[2]

How many brothers did the rich man have?

Sweet says he had *six* brothers.

Lazarus was *also* his brother. Not his literal blood brother, but a fellow son of God. Lazarus sat outside his gate every day and the rich man *never* invited him in to eat with him. The rich man considered Lazarus barely worth his table scraps. He didn't see him as a brother and *that* is why he is in hell.

I think Len is right in his take on the parable. The Scriptures are clear that the poor are our brothers and sisters. If you didn't pick up on it in my story, "Pedro" is the ghost of John's brother PJ, come back from Hades to warn him about his impending fate. Like the rich man, we must learn to see the poor as our brothers and sisters.

When you help others, it is easy to take the position of benefactor and treat the poor as less than. The kingdom of God pushes back on this posture. All wealth is God's; we are merely stewards. God challenges us to see the poor as brothers and sisters and to treat them accordingly.

2. Luke 16:28.

In 1 Corinthians 10, Paul challenges the Corinthian rich and poor to see each other as brothers and sisters. Using the Lord's Supper as an illustration, he says: "The cup of blessing that we bless, is it not a participation in the blood of Christ? The bread that we break, is it not a participation in the body of Christ? Because there is one bread, we who are many are one body, for we all partake of the one bread."[3]

The shared bread reminds us that we are *all*—rich and poor, Jew and gentile, slave and free—*one* body of Christ. Jesus is the firstborn and one day we will dine together in the kingdom of God.

QUESTIONS FOR REFLECTION

1. What is one word that you would use to describe the relationship between siblings (the way they *should* be)?

2. What do you think about Jesus' story of the rich man and Lazarus? Do you like how it ends? If you could change it at all, how would you have it end?

3. Read through the parable of Jesus again—how would you describe the rich man's attitude toward Lazarus (even in Hades!)?

4. What could the rich man have done differently?

5. Who are some people (beyond just the poor) that we tend to treat as "less than"?

6. What are some ways that we can honor the dignity of those we help? How do we treat people as brothers and sisters despite their life situation?

---

3. 1 Corinthians 10:16–17.

Visuals

"And we know that for those who love God all things work together for good, for those who are called according to his purpose." (Romans 8:28)

LOOKS CAN BE DECEIVING. Isn't that what they always say? Kindergarteners learn the old adage, "you can't judge a book by its cover," but then they spend the rest of their lives judging books by their covers.

I used to pride myself in my keen dust-jacket discernment. That's why I went into sales. I thought I could look at a person and judge within seconds how to close the deal. But Rick Anderson taught me that I didn't know as much as I thought I knew.

It all started when Rick called me into his office to talk about a potential deal with Helios, an emerging renewable energy company. Rick and I worked for a database company called Surpass, and Helios was looking for some new software.

"Allen!" he greeted me as I entered his office. "Have a seat."

Rick was a legend in my industry. People said that he could sell a whale burger to a vegan member of Green Peace. Now in the twilight of his career, Rick had been relegated to corporate training. He was supposed to mentor the rest of us sales guys—give us feedback and help us improve our presentations.

It was kind of sad to see Rick behind a desk, trapped in a cage disguised as a corner office. Watching him train young salespeople was like watching a lion do tricks at the zoo—he was impressive, but you couldn't help but feel he was meant for the wild.

That being said, Rick made the most of his position at Surpass. He was from the old school—forever faithful to the company and free from the vainglory of youth. I think Rick's only ambitions were to work hard and to help the company succeed. If that meant sales—he'd sell. If that meant teaching others to sell—that was just fine with him, too. Whatever Surpass needed from him, he was willing and able to do.

I think the corporate bigwigs knew that Rick was a salesman at heart, so they still threw him a bone once in a while. They let him chase an occasional lead if the payoff was big enough. I was guessing that this was what the Helios lead was—renewable energy is the future, and a deal with Helios could pay huge dividends later. That being said, I was sure that everybody would be after them and it would be a tough sell.

I surveyed my surroundings as I sat down opposite Rick. His desk was immaculate—just a monitor, a calendar, an inbox, and a picture of his grandkids. The rest of his office was equally tidy. Funky bright oil paintings hung on the wall, giving it a sophisticated but welcoming look. A bookshelf in the corner displayed titles ranging from Charles Dickens's *A Tale of Two*

Cities to Malcolm Gladwell's *Blink* and Rick Warren's *The Purpose Driven Life*. He even had an espresso maker tucked away in its proper place.

"Thanks for meeting with me, Allen," Rick said with a smile. "You're having quite a quarter!"

"Thanks," I tried to say modestly.

"What's your secret?"

"A good teacher," I said.

"Huh. I don't know about that. You're a gifted young man, Allen. Don't think we haven't noticed that."

"Thanks," I said again. I didn't know how else to respond.

I sat there in silence for a second before Rick changed the subject. "I'd like your help with something, Allen. I've got a sales call with Helios this weekend. This could be a huge. But Greg can't go with me, so I need a new partner. Would you fill in for him? Nailing this contract could be big for you."

He was right. This was the kind of deal that would really put me over the top. I had good numbers, but my sales partner Javier was integral to my success. He was fantastic. He designed the presentations; I did the talking. On more than one occasion, a prospective client interrupted my presentation to see one of his graphic demonstrations a second time. He definitely brought the "wow" to the team.

Showing the suits that I could hang with the top sales guys like Rick would remove any doubts they had about me. It would show them that I could work without Javier and it would secure me as the go-to guy at Surpass. Plus, I could tell that this deal was important to Rick. He'd be a good ally to have going forward.

On the other hand, I wasn't sure I *could* work with anyone other than Javier. A lot of my success was due to our chemistry. I knew what to expect from his aids, and he knew where I would go with the presentation. Could I duplicate my part without Javier?

"Wow," I finally said to Rick. "I'm flattered that you thought of me. That's quite an opportunity."

"I thought of you right away," he replied. "I think you're ready for this."

I leaned forward in my chair enthusiastically. "Well, it will be different not working with Javier, but I want to do it. I think we can make it work."

"Great," he said. "My work is a bit different from Javier's, but I can give you the stuff so you can familiarize yourself with it before we go."

"Oh great," I said. "That would be fantastic."

He pulled a flash drive out of his desk, loaded some files on to it, and then handed it to me. "Can you be ready to leave tomorrow night? The meeting is on Thursday."

"Of course," I said. "I'll take a look at your stuff tonight and I'll be ready by tomorrow."

"I'm looking forward to it."

***

I walked down the hall after leaving Rick's office, and I did a little fist pump as soon as I was sure no one was watching. This was incredible! It was going to be my moment of glory. Rick and I were going to nail this deal, and my career was going to take off.

I wasted no time getting to work when I got home. I grabbed a sandwich and ate it in front of the computer as I loaded up Rick's presentation files. Javier was good, but I was on pins and needles anticipating what Rick's stuff would look like.

The first file I ran was a demonstration of our customizable reports. I double-clicked the video file and waited as it opened. A couple seconds later, a low-resolution demonstration of an outdated version began to play. It had narration—bad narration. The file was low resolution, and when the report finally generated, it looked terrible. Surely Rick didn't actually use this file in presentations. He must have mixed a training exercise up with a real file.

I ended the video and looked for another file to try. He had a Power-Point slideshow comparing the functionality of our software to that of the competitors. I opened it and gasped at what I saw. The background was cheesy and the font was unreadable. I clicked through the slideshow and the program froze. That couldn't be real.

I browsed through the rest of the material on the flash drive. It was all equally bad. In fact, it was disastrous. I shut everything down and stared at my monitor in disbelief. Was this a mistake? It had to be. Rick was a legend. How could he work with such bad material? Were the stories about him all myths? What was going on?

I decided to call Rick and ask him about the visual aids. Maybe it wasn't too late to make some changes. If nothing else, maybe we could use Javier's stuff. I reached for the phone and then hesitated. How was I going to confront Rick about this? I couldn't get on his bad side. That would be career suicide. But neither could I go in to a presentation with this stuff. It was awful. We needed to talk.

I decided to make the call. Rick answered after a few rings. "Hello?" he said.

"Hey Rick? This is Allen. I'm sorry to call you at home. I didn't interrupt anything, did I?"

"No, of course not," he said. "What's up?" He was cheerful as ever.

"Well, I've been going through the visual aids that you gave me, and I was wondering if we could make some changes."

"Why? What's wrong with them?" he asked, suddenly sounding concerned.

"Well, maybe I'm just used to Javier's work, but the resolution on the video files is pretty low, and I'm having a hard time reading the PowerPoints."

"Yeah, I know Javier uses higher resolution video than I do, but my videos work pretty well. I don't think we need to change anything."

"I am sure that your presentations work great," I said, "but I wonder if they could be even better if we used some sharper visuals."

"I see what you're saying, Allen, but I think we're okay. I've been using this stuff for years and I've closed a lot of big deals. Can you trust me on this one? I know what I'm doing."

He had a point. He *had* been around for a while. But still, there was no way this stuff was going to work. I needed to press him for a change. "I believe you, Rick," I assured him. "You're the best. But you know, sometimes we get so used to looking at something that we stop noticing ways it can be improved. Maybe I can just call Javier and get his stuff."

"You don't need to do that. We're good with what we have." His tone was suddenly stern. "If you're not comfortable working without Javier, I can look for someone else..."

I cut him off. "That's unnecessary, Rick. I can work with this. Maybe I've just gotten so used to working with Javier that anything different seems wrong. I'll just spend some more time looking at your stuff. It'll come to me."

"Great," Rick replied. "Anything else?"

"No. That's it. Thanks for your help, Rick. Have a good night."

"Good night," he said, hanging up.

I sat there in my chair in front of the computer, phone in hand. What was I going to do? Rick's stuff was awful. There was no way I could close a deal with it. But I needed to use it. There was no feasible alternative. Maybe if I stepped up *my* game, I could compensate for Rick. But what could I do differently? And how could I improve on such short notice?

I broke out a legal pad and started brainstorming ways to improve my presentation. I decided to use as little of Rick's monstrous visual aids as possible so as to lessen their impact. I worked through the night and into the early morning memorizing statistics and selling points. I also researched everything I could about Helios, looking for any inside information or angle of approach for my presentation. I even researched the people I was meeting with—who they were, where they had come from, and what they were about. I was surprised at what I was able to find.

I guess I had just assumed that the guys at Helios would be a bunch of tree-huggers. But I was wrong; they were more than that. Sure, they were ecologically responsible, but they approached green technology from a fiscal standpoint. They believed that the future of the global economy was renewable energy, and they wanted their company to be at the front of the next economic boom. Maybe this deal *could* be salvaged.

***

I woke up the next morning to the alarm of my cell phone. I had fallen asleep at my computer. My mind was in a haze after such a long night, but I wasn't going to let *that* deter me. A little coffee could get me through the day. Still, my fatigue brewed some resentment toward Rick. He'd been in the industry a long time. He was a legend. I shouldn't have to pull all-nighters to compensate for his poor work. But, what was I going to do? My career demanded I close this deal and stay on Rick's good side. I tried to bury my resentment as I prepared for the day and the trip ahead.

My work day wasn't much better than my morning. Try as I might, I couldn't shake my anger toward Rick. It's not that I thought we'd botch the sales call (I thought we had a chance); it was that my extra work was going to win the day, but Rick's reputation was going to blind everyone to my success.

Rick and I shared a cab to the airport after work and then sat next to each other on the plane. It was hard for me to mask my annoyance with him, especially since he was so chatty during the flight. It was like he was either oblivious or apathetic to his shortcomings.

The more time I spent with Rick, the more I began to question his reputation. How did he establish himself as such a salesman? His work was terrible, and he didn't seem to realize it. Maybe his sales partner was fantastic. Maybe Rick's charisma made him *seem* better than he really was. Maybe his theoretical expertise overshadowed his practical ineptitude. I couldn't figure it out.

Rick and I checked into our hotel, and I stayed up again doing research. I wanted to make sure that I was as prepared as possible for what was ahead. The next morning, we ate breakfast together to work out the last-minute details before our big meeting.

We sat down in a four-person booth at this greasy-spoon near the hotel. All around us were business people just like us—all dressed in the same dark suits and power ties, all drinking coffee to mask whatever they had done the night before, all psyching each other up over western omelets, French toast, or biscuits and gravy.

I felt like a ferret was running wild in my stomach. Two straight nights of less than four hours' sleep were taking a toll on me. I could have lay down right there in the booth and used the oversized plastic menu as a blanket. Rick looked chipper as ever. He obviously didn't stay up late to prepare the night before. He brought the morning paper in one hand and his laptop in the other. We ordered our food and started to discuss the meeting ahead.

"You ready?" he asked me over his coffee. His tone was like that of a father talking to a nervous third grader about to play his first Pop Warner football game.

"Yeah, I'm good to go," I replied shortly. "I've been doing a lot of research over the past few nights. I think we've got a good chance."

Rick leaned forward in his booth. "Yeah, you seem like you really prepared for this call. Do you normally work this hard?"

I was taken back by his remark. Was he questioning my work ethic? I'd seen his visual aids—he wasn't exactly a perfectionist himself. I even told him *specific* things that he could improve, and he ignored my input. How could he expect me to take his advice seriously when he wasn't willing to change something that was so obviously flawed? I took a deep breath before I responded. Now was not the time for an angry rant. "Well, I always prepare, but I *have* put more into this call than normal. I really want to nail this."

Rick smiled. "Good. You're going to be great," he assured me. I laughed to myself. Thanks Rick, that means *so* much, I thought. You obviously spend *so* much time refining your technique.

"I hope you don't mind," Rick interrupted my mental tirade, "but I made a couple of changes to the presentation." He opened his laptop as he spoke.

My interest piqued. "Oh yeah?" I asked. "What kind of changes?"

"Well, I thought about the feedback you gave my presentation," he said. "I think you were right. Some of my visuals were a little sloppy. I redid them, and I think these new ones are better. I brought them along with me so that we could go over them before the meeting."

I was taken aback again. He redid his presentation at my advice? Rick turned his laptop toward me and proceeded to show me a completely different collection of videos and slideshows. They looked nothing like the batch he gave me earlier. In fact, they were *fantastic*. The videos were crisp. The slideshows were sharp. The graphics were beautiful. They were perfect.

He even showed me this video he created tracing the effects our software had on our five biggest clients. Clean, clear, convincing graphs showed how our product increased efficiency, decreased user errors, and saved each company millions in labor and mistakes. Even *I* was impressed by the video, and I *knew* all of that information. Where did all of this come from?

"Rick..." I started, "I don't know what to say. These look fantastic. How did you have time to make these changes?"

He winked at me. "I told you I'd get it done." He looked at his watch. "Oh! We need to go," he said, closing his laptop and gathering his things. "We don't want to be late." He called for the check and we were off to the meeting.

***

I was quiet the whole way to Helios. I couldn't get over Rick's improved presentation. I had never seen anything so good. How did he come up with that, and in such short time? I couldn't believe it. Maybe there *was* something to his reputation.

I went into the meeting with new confidence. I was already sure of my speaking skills, but armed with Rick's graphics, I knew we would blow them away. True to my prediction, they were impressed. I could see the awe in their eyes as we showed them how much Helios could benefit from our software. I was prepared for all of their questions, and I was able to bring every answer back to their company's goals and core values. I couldn't have asked for a better experience. When I finished, the execs at Helios asked if we wouldn't mind giving them a minute to talk things over. They wanted to make a decision right away, but they wanted to discuss it before they gave us an answer. Rick and I excused ourselves into the hallway.

"Fantastic job, Allen," Rick said as soon as we were alone. "I think you nailed this."

"Thanks. I think they were impressed by our presentation." Rick looked giddy. I had to admit, I was pretty excited myself.

"I have to ask, Rick," I said after a few seconds of silence. "How did you make such dramatic improvements to your visuals in such a short time frame?"

He grinned as he considered his response. "I told you to trust me," was all he said.

"I should have listened," I said, smiling and shaking my head at myself. "If I had known how good you were, I could have saved myself a lot of trouble!"

"What do you mean?"

"Well, I kind of panicked when I saw your original work. I convinced myself that I needed to prepare a lot more if we were going to close this deal. I put a lot more work than I needed to."

"Is that so?" he said. "Well, as long as it is confession time, I have one, too. I never planned to use those files I gave you originally."

"What?! Why would you do that to me? It's funny; I was convinced you had lost it. Maybe you had too much time behind a desk and not enough time on calls. I was starting to think that the rumors about you were untrue. Why wouldn't you give me the best right away?"

Before he had time to answer, the guys from Helios called us back into the conference room. We went in and sat down. Five of their managers and executives stared back at us from the other side of the table, smiling.

"We love what you guys do," the guy in the middle with the gray suit said. "Your software outperforms all the competition at a comparable price. We think we need to move on this quickly for the future of our company. Do we have a deal?"

"Of course," Rick chimed in, extending his hand to the executive from Helios.

"Great. On a side note, I want you guys to know that you're not the only company to meet with us about database software. We've received a number of bids on this project. But your presentation this morning set you guys apart. Not only was it clear and streamlined, but you two really seemed to understand our company. I can tell that you two put a lot of work into making sure that your product was right for us." He looked at me as he spoke. "It means a lot to us that you put in the extra time to find out what we're about."

Rick made some closing arrangements with the guys from Helios, and we ordered a formal proposal to be sent right away. We all shook hands and then we were on our way.

I was beaming. They were clear that the extra work I did was integral to us landing that deal. Rick had to understand that. I was already dreaming about what this might do for my career as we left Helios' office.

"Rick, you never answered my question," I said. "Why didn't you give me your best presentation right away?" I was as confused about him as ever.

He smiled as I spoke, and then he asked a penetrating question. He looked me right in the eyes and said, "If I had, would you have prepared to the extent that made that sale?"

I stopped in my tracks as his words hit me. Wow. He was right. I *wouldn't* have prepared as much. And we wouldn't have made that sale. I shook my head in disbelief as I started walking again.

Rick followed up. "I wasn't blowing smoke when I said you're great at what you do. You *are* great. And I think you can be even better. But you have a problem—your sales partner Javier is fantastic, and as long as you're his partner, you're never going to have to stretch yourself to make a big sale. I challenged you to stretch you, and you rose to the occasion. I am proud of you."

"Thanks," I said, snickering. I was embarrassed at being played, but I knew he was right. There was a reason Rick was where he was.

We talked for hours on the flight home about sales, my technique, and my potential. My anger at Rick was long gone, and it had been replaced by wonder. Rick *was* the best. He genuinely cared for me, and he had been watching me for quite some time. This lesson had been a long time in the making, because Rick thought I was worth it.

Looking back, I can't believe I doubted Rick in the first place. He had a plan all along. After that day, I never second-guessed him. There were times when he would say or do things that made me think he had finally lost his mind. But he always had a reason for the things that didn't make sense. When all was said and done, he always left me looking back thinking, "Of course. How could it have been any other way?"

"He put another parable before them, saying, 'The kingdom of heaven may be compared to a man who sowed good seed in his field, but while his men were sleeping, his enemy came and sowed weeds among the wheat and went away. So when the plants came up and bore grain, then the weeds appeared also. And the servants of the master of the house came and said to him, "Master, did you not sow good seed in your field? How then does it have weeds?" He said to them, "An enemy has done this." So the servants said to him, "Then do you want us to go and gather them?" But he said, "No, lest in gathering the weeds you root up the wheat along with them. Let both grow together until the harvest, and at harvest time I will tell the reapers, 'Gather the weeds first and bind them in bundles to be burned, but gather the wheat into my barn.'''''' (Matthew 13:24–30)*

IN LUKE 4, JESUS famously enters a synagogue and reads the long-hoped-for words from the prophet Isaiah: "The Spirit of the Lord is upon me, because he has anointed me to proclaim good news to the poor. He has sent me to proclaim liberty to the captives and recovering of sight to the blind, to set at liberty those who are oppressed, to proclaim the year of the Lord's favor."[1] He then rolls up the scroll, looks around the room and says, "Today's the day, folks. God's work starts *today*."

God promised good news for the poor. He promised liberty for the captives, sight for the spiritually blind, and freedom for the oppressed. Those are powerful words, but anyone listening in that synagogue that day would look around and say, "Uh, Jesus—we're still poor. Rome still rules over us. We're still oppressed. Death still reigns. If the kingdom of God is at hand, what kind of king do we have?"

Not much has changed since then. The problem of evil has long been the most damaging philosophical argument against Christianity. Simply stated, an all-loving God would want to prevent evil, an all-knowing God would know of its existence, and an all-powerful God would be able to prevent it. Thus, if evil exists, then an all-knowing, all-powerful, all-loving God cannot exist.

1. Luke 4:18–19.

When we look at the world around us, it's clear something is not right. Some people look at that and see proof that God doesn't exist. Jesus looked at it and he saw proof that God wasn't done yet. Right now, there is good and there is evil. But this isn't the end of the story—someday God will make right all that has been made wrong.

This is similar to what Allen went through in my story. Allen had heard the stories about Rick and how good he was, but when he saw Rick's work, he thought, *something is not right here.* When Allen confronted Rick, Rick did nothing. All along, Rick was aware of the problem. He wanted to fix it, and he was able to fix it—but he didn't fix it. This left Allen scratching his head in disbelief. *Maybe the stories are untrue,* he thought. *Maybe Rick isn't as good as people say he is.* But in the end, Rick fixed what needed to be fixed, and he made clear his reasons for temporarily leaving it unfixed.

In Romans 8, Paul tells us, "And we know that for those who love God all things work together for good, for those who are called according to his purpose."[2] This verse has been abused over the years. It doesn't mean that *each and every* thing that happens results in good, but rather that we can be confident that in the end, it's all going to work out. God is in control. He is going to defeat evil.

It has been my experience that most people aren't as bothered by hypothetical evil as they are by the *real* evil that they have experienced. Our doubts aren't *philosophical*; they're *personal*. We understand that bad things *can* happen, we just wish they wouldn't happen to us. We wonder why God *lets* them happen to us.

I don't have an answer to that question. I think it is okay to be angry about the things you have suffered. Jesus says in the parable that *an enemy* sowed the weeds. The weeds weren't a part of the original plan. They're foreign. If there is a God like the one Jesus described, then we have a reason to be upset over evil and injustice. But if we're all alone, then we have no reason for indignation. We have no reason to expect anything but survival of the fittest and the cold indifference of nature.

It is significant that in the interpretation of the parable of the wheat and the weeds, Jesus never tells us what the purpose of evil is. We should never presume to know what we're not told. But, one day we'll know, and it will all make sense. Until then, we're left in suspense.

When my wife was pregnant with my daughter Avery, we tried our best to imagine what she might look like. Would she have my eyes? Would

2. Romans 8:28.

she have Brooke's cheeks? What color would her hair be? Would she look more like mom or like dad? We were left in suspense.

But I'll never forget the first time I saw Avery, and it all made sense. I saw her chubby little cheeks, and her nose that looks just like her brother's, and her toes that looked like mine, and I thought, *Of course! Of course that's what she looks like. How could she look any different?*

We're not told why God allowed evil. But we're told that God is working it for good, and one day we'll know. One day, when God has made the world right, and there is no more sickness, no more death, no more injustice, we'll look back at the world and what God did with it and we'll think, *Of course! Of course that's the way it had to be. How could it have been any different?*

QUESTIONS FOR REFLECTION

1. Have you ever misjudged someone? What did you initially think and how were you proven wrong?

2. What is your immediate reaction to this parable? Have you ever thought about evil this way?

3. What evil things about the world (war, poverty, injustice) bother you the most? What do you wish God would do?

4. Have you ever endured something hard only to have a good result? What did you endure and how did it bring about good?

5. What do you think about the significance of "the enemy" sowing the weeds in the field? Does that make a difference to you when you think about evil?

6. How can we better remind ourselves every day that God is good, and he is in control?

Diesel

"And let us not grow weary of doing good, for in due season we will reap, if we do not give up." (Galatians 6:9)

I'VE NEVER BEEN A quitter. You can call me a lot of things—impulsive, competitive, narcissistic—but you can't call me a quitter. I *never* quit. Okay, there was one time that I *almost* quit, but even on that occasion I was able to outlast the competition. I don't quit.

The time I almost quit was about two years ago. After a great holiday season, I showed up to work ready for a new year and a fresh start. I was going to get both. Christmas had been great because I was able to go home to be with my family. Then, I came back to Indiana for a fantastic New Year's Eve party at my friend Chris's house. I couldn't have asked for a better week.

But I was feeling a little sluggish on my first day back on the job. Maybe it was the extra helpings of pumpkin pie, the Christmas cookies I kept sneaking, or that extra glass of champagne I swore I wasn't going to drink. I felt like I had gained five pounds over the week. Whatever the reason, I was dragging.

I was a few minutes late on my first day back. By the time I got there, the team was already busy working. Kurt was eating a bowl of oatmeal as he input numbers into a database. Jen and Daphne were chatting away about last week's snow, and how Daphne's poor husband almost had a heart attack digging their car out. These guys were great. The four of us did all of the administrative work for the Elliot Brothers Mortgage Company outside of Indianapolis. We were a well-oiled machine, and yet we managed to have fun along the way.

"Good morning, Michael. How were the holidays?" asked Daphne.

"Great," I said. "It's always good to go home for Christmas."

"Amen to that," she said with her typical cheer. I loved Daphne. Everyone loved Daphne. In fact, I don't think it was possible *not* to love Daphne. She was one of those people who always smiles, no matter what is going on in life. She always had a laugh, always an encouragement. Her cube was covered with pictures of dogs and cats caught in funny poses with captions in doge speak. I wondered how she managed to stay so upbeat all of the time. Then again, sometimes her joy felt forced, like deep down she felt she *had* to smile. And whenever I was in a bad mood, her chipper attitude was maddening. Plus, she was the flightiest person I had ever met. She always had some new fad diet or some new miracle vitamin. When you asked what happened to *last* week's diet, she would laugh and say, "Oh, I'm *over* that." How could you not love Daphne?

"You know, I love to see my parents around the holidays, but I can't stop eating when I'm there. I had a hard time finding a pair of pants that fit this morning," I said.

"That's what the holidays are for," Kurt said to Daphne's delight.

Kurt had the cube next to Daphne. He was the veteran of the group, having been at Elliot Brothers since the early nineties. He knew everything about our jobs—why we did things the way we did, how we did them back in 1992, and why we changed. Kurt was great. We needed him. But he also had a cynical side, and convincing him to change was almost impossible.

I felt like Kurt had a story—like he used to have hopes and dreams, but they were crushed by someone or something, so he settled for sitting at the same cube every morning, eating oatmeal out of the same bowl. I'd almost asked him on a dozen occasions what he was like when he was younger, but then he'd glare at me over the top of his glasses and I'd figure that door should probably stay closed.

He may have been a bit of a curmudgeon, but he had a good heart. Every office needs a Kurt.

"Maybe we could all use a few less holidays, then," said Jen, smugly.

Jen was new to the team, having started only a few months ago, and we were still getting used to her. She was tough to read. She seemed nice enough, but she also knew how to take the wind out of a conversation's sails. She was a do-gooder, and you could always count on her to remind you of the life lessons you learned in Sunday school. She was good, and yet there was a sadness in her eyes that suggested more to her—like the look a sailor gets when he's been on land too long. It's like she longed for a distant country and a better life, but was imprisoned in a tiny cube in an insignificant office in a no-name hamlet outside of a mid-sized Bible-belt city. It never seemed like she was *there*, even when she was there.

I'm thinking of getting back in shape now that the holidays are over," Jen continued. "I used to exercise all the time, but it's been hard since moving here. It's so cold and windy!"

"Why don't you join a gym?" Daphne asked. "That way you don't have to worry about the weather as much."

"Yeah, that's what I'll probably do," Jen said with a sigh. She was getting that look again, like she was somewhere else.

"You know," Daphne started, "I saw this billboard on I-70 for a new gym that's opening in town. The guy who runs it is named Diesel McDaniels, and apparently he's really good. He used to work in Los Angeles and he knows all of the secrets the stars use to stay in shape."

I rolled my eyes. "You and your Hollywood exercise plans..."

"No, seriously," she replied. "I've heard this guy is good. You should come, too, Michael."

I looked down at my midsection. Maybe some more exercise *would* be good for me. But I didn't need some muscle head to tell me how to get into shape. I ran track in high school. I knew how to take care of myself.

"Maybe we could all go together!" Jen burst out. "Wouldn't that be cool if we all met at the gym before coming to work? It would help us all get off to a good start."

"That would be so cool!" Daphne shouted. It didn't take much to convince her. I have to admit, the thought of getting up an hour earlier to hit the weights with these guys didn't seem like my idea of a party. Unless...

"We could have a contest," I suggested gleefully. We could talk to this Diesel McSixpack guy and then see who can lose the most weight.

"I love that idea," Daphne said. I knew she would.

"I don't know," Jen said. "I don't think we need to make it a competition. I was thinking more of our health—"

"I think a competition would be fun," I said. "We could all pitch in 100 dollars, and if you miss a workout, you are out of the contest. The last man standing, errr, the last *person* standing wins the money." I really did mean last *man* standing. I knew I would win.

"I don't see why it has to be a competition," Jen said. "I think we should focus on health. What do *you* think Kurt?"

Kurt looked up from his computer screen. He had a blank look on his face and oatmeal on his shirt. "Oh, I don't care. I'm not much of an exerciser, but maybe a contest would motivate me."

"It's a deal, then!" I declared. "We'll go talk to Diesel on Monday and make a workout plan. Everyone chip in 100 dollars, and the last person to miss a workout gets the pot." Everyone agreed, and the bet was on.

***

That next week we all met at Diesel's gym at 6:00 a.m. We were all a bit groggy, but I think the excitement of a new workout routine superseded our fatigue. Diesel showed us into his office, where he proceeded to explain his workout routine to us. He called it D-3X—D for Diesel, and three for the three main areas his routine emphasized—chest and triceps, back and biceps, and legs and abs. I don't know what the X stood for; he probably just threw it in at the end to make it sound more extreme.

Diesel's office was comical. A massive bookshelf dominated the back wall, but there wasn't a single book on it. Instead, it was filled with trophies—wrestling, swimming, cross-country, boxing, tai kwon do, and, of course, weight lifting. This guy was a machine. The other office walls were full of autographed pictures of celebrities. He was too much.

"So, what brings you to see the Diesel today?" he barked. I couldn't help but laugh to myself. Not only did he refer to himself in the third person, but he even put an article in front of his name. Was this guy for real?

"We want to get buff!" Daphne said, flexing her bicep.

"Well, you've come to the right place," Diesel retorted with authority. "The Diesel can whip you softies into shape in no time. What are we looking for—cardio? Weight loss? Muscle building?"

"All of it!" Daphne shouted. She was like a kid talking to Santa Claus.

"All right," Diesel said. "I like the energy. We can do all of that here with my D-3X program. But are you guys up for the task? 'Cause I don't mess around. If you're going to train with me, you're going to work. If you're just here to play games, I'm not interested in working with you. I only want to train you if you want to change."

We all looked at each other. I *thought* we were serious. But this guy took serious to a whole new level.

Jen said, "Diesel, I think we're all looking to change. What we're doing now just isn't working, and we want to be healthier. I think I can speak for the group when I say that we are willing to put in the work."

Maybe Jen would be tougher competition than I thought.

"Good." Diesel said, nodding at Jen with a smile. "I'm glad you're committed, because change hurts. My motto is 'pain is weakness leaving the body.' The more it hurts, the more you are purging yourself of the old you."

Pain is weakness leaving the body? I knew I liked this guy. Kurt was going to have a heart attack. Daphne was going to cry. And Jen, well Jen better think long and hard about what she's getting into competing against me.

Diesel droned on about the intensity of his workout and the pain that we were in for. He told us that he wasn't there to be our friend or to help us achieve some new level of zen. He was there to discipline us—to show us the way so we could help ourselves. He warned us that if we were looking for someone to do the work for us, then we needed to go somewhere else.

Diesel finished his diatribe against wussiness and handed out waiver forms for each of us to sign. We stared at each other in shock. Kurt looked like he was going to be sick. Daphne had a huge grin on her face. Jen was smiling confidently. I think she thought she could win this contest.

"Do we really have to sign this?" Kurt asked.

"Absolutely." Diesel growled. "I need to know that you are in good medical condition and you aren't going to hold me responsible if you bite off more than you can chew."

"It says in paragraph three that there is a risk of broken bones, cardiac episode, stroke, or even death. Could those things really happen?"

"Why would it say that if it they couldn't?" Diesel said matter-of-factly. "True life change demands risk and hard work. If you're not willing to take the risk or do the work, then you're not ready to change." Diesel stared at Kurt like a Doberman at a squirrel. Kurt looked terrified.

"Yeah, guys, I don't think I'm ready for all of this," Kurt said nervously. "My heart isn't what it used to be, and I don't want to get hurt. I am certainly not signing this waiver."

"Come on, Kurt. It's not going to be the same without you!" said Daphne. We all pleaded with Kurt to give it a try, but he was adamant.

"Let him go," Diesel finally commanded. "The path to change is painful. Anyone who walks in these doors and looks back isn't worthy of the D-3X. If he doesn't really want to change, let him go."

We all looked at Diesel in fear and disbelief. What were we getting ourselves into?

"It's okay, guys," Kurt assured us. "I am sorry I couldn't be a better workout partner. But this is too much for me. I want you to keep my 100 dollars for the winner."

At that, he stood up and left. "Do we still want to do this?" Jen asked, obviously sad over Kurt's departure.

"Absolutely," I said. "Kurt wants us to keep going. So, it wasn't for him. That doesn't mean that we can't work together."

Jen and Daphne both smiled. "Okay," Jen said. "Let's do it."

We signed all the paperwork and then Diesel oriented us to the facility and the exercises we would be doing. This was going to be the easiest 400 dollars I ever made. I figured Diesel would break these two princesses before month's end. The carnage was going to be glorious.

***

As it turns out, I was *half* right. The next day, we started working with Diesel. He was not kidding about the program's intensity. By the week's end, I hurt in ways I didn't know I could. I spent most of Saturday morning limping around my apartment. Yet, at the same time, I felt stronger already. I certainly felt that I could outlast my coworkers. If *I* was hurting like this, imagine what *they* must be going through.

I got to the gym early on Monday morning, wanting the competition to know that I was ready for another round. Jen showed up shortly after me, confident as ever. "Good to see you made it through the weekend," she said with a smile. "I wasn't sure I was going to see you this morning."

"Wouldn't miss it for the world," I said. We waited for about fifteen minutes for Daphne to show. Somehow, I knew she wasn't going to be here. She *had* to be in pain. When it was clear that Daphne wasn't coming, Jen said, "Well, I guess it's just you and me. Ready?" I was.

Daphne was fifteen minutes late for work that day, in obvious pain. "Morning guys," she winced as she walked in the door. "How was the workout?"

"Great!" I said. "Never felt better in my life."

"Daphne, we missed you," Jen corrected. "It wasn't the same without you."

"Yeah. I had a rocky weekend. The workout was too much for me! I'm sorry I let you guys down, but I can barely walk! I don't think I'm cut out for the D-3X."

I gave Jen an assured smile. It was down to just the two of us. She forced a smile in return. One week into the contest, and half of the competition had folded. How long would Jen last? Two weeks? Three? It was going to be fun to watch her fold under the pressure.

But she didn't fold. In fact, she seemed to get stronger as the days turned into weeks and weeks turned into months. We both stuck it out for six months without missing a workout, and we were seeing great results. My love handles were starting to go away and I could see the muscles in my stomach for the first time in my life. Diesel's workout routine was fantastic, and I was pleased with what I was seeing.

That being said, the contest was also harder on me than I ever thought it would be. I had a couple of close calls after I was up late watching TV and had to fight the temptation to sleep in the next day.

Further, things were getting busier at work, a great new sports bar opened up near my apartment, and Chris had got me hooked on this new online video game. Between work, hanging out with friends, and unwinding at my apartment, it was becoming harder to squeeze time into my schedule for a workout. The contest was quickly becoming a thorn in my side.

Five months in, I was starting to fear I might lose. Life was just too hectic to keep going. Fortunately, Jen provided an escape when she announced that she had been offered a great position at another office across town. This was just what I needed.

On her last day at the office, I tried to weasel my way into a draw.

"So, this is the end." I said to her regretfully.

"Yeah," she said. "I'm going to miss this place. I really liked working with you guys."

I could tell by the look in her eyes that she was sincere. She really was going to miss it.

"I bet you're going to miss our workouts with Diesel, too," I added.

"You know," she said, "I thought I might keep up with those. I mean, it's been good for us." She reached over and squeezed my bicep playfully.

I was taken aback by her words. I had assumed that she would be done with the contest since she was leaving the office. If she kept working out, I don't know how much longer I could keep going. I was down to five hours of sleep every night, and getting up in the morning had become a chore. In fact, the only thing keeping me going was the thought that she would be quitting soon so I only needed to stick with it a few more days.

"It *has* been good for us." I laughed nervously. "But, don't you feel that you've accomplished all your goals? I mean, you've really trimmed down. I don't know about you, but I feel like this could be a good stopping point for the contest. Maybe we can call it a draw?"

"Well, it's not just about the contest," Jen said. She looked down at her feet. "You know, I thought it would be a neat way for us to keep seeing each other when I'm gone. I've really enjoyed our time together."

Oh no. She wasn't going to quit. She wanted to beat me so bad that she was going to keep the workout going after moving to a new job. Really? Was she *that* competitive?

"Yeah, the contest has been fun. But I'm not sure how much longer I want to do it. I'm happy with the results I've seen, and so much stuff has come up in my life that I haven't been sleeping very much. I just think I'm ready for something new."

I saw sadness come over Jen's face. "You want to quit?" she asked.

She really wanted to keep going. I realized then that there was no way I was going to win. I was done, and she looked like she had a whole reservoir of energy. I couldn't believe it, but she was going to beat me.

"I've got so much going on—"

"Like what?" she interrupted.

"Well... work... and stuff. I don't know. I can never seem to get to bed before midnight. There's just too much going on."

"What if you stopped watching TV, or stopped going out with Chris all the time. I bet you'd find a lot more time to sleep then. You don't *have* to quit. Please?"

Did she just rebuke me for wasting time? Who did she think she was? She didn't know me, and she didn't know my life. I was busy, and this contest was choking me. "I'm not going to quit before you," I jabbed. "I don't quit at anything, and I'm going to beat you."

She was silent. "You're still thinking about the contest?"

"What? Like you're not. I know you want to beat me."

Jen looked even sadder. She stood there in silence for a minute and then said, "You know Michael, it was never about the contest for me—it was about making changes. It was about becoming the person I wanted to be. And it was about spending time with someone I cared about. The contest was just something silly to get me started. Are you really just doing this for the contest?"

"Well, no. Not *just* for the contest. I mean, I wanted to get into shape." I didn't know what to say. We stood there for another minute or two, before she finally said, "Well, it was nice working with you. Thanks for everything you've done for me." She hugged me, then turned and left.

***

I was up late again that night, and I had trouble sleeping. How was I going to beat this girl? She was too strong, too determined. I tossed and turned all night worrying about the prospect of quitting.

I woke up the next morning feeling worse than ever. That was it. I was done. I couldn't keep going like this. She beat me. But I decided I wasn't going to give her the glory of a no-show. I was going to get dressed, go to the gym, and forfeit in person.

I put my clothes on and headed to the gym. I arrived a few minutes late, but well within the parameters of the contest. But Jen was nowhere to be seen. I waited for her to show up, practicing my concession speech. I stood there for about five minutes before one of the guys behind the desk called me over. "Michael?"

"Yeah," I said.

"The woman you work out with was here earlier and she left something for you."

I walked over to the desk, and he handed me an envelope. I opened it, and inside was 400 dollars and a note. All it said was, "Congratulations."

She quit. Why did she quit? It must have been something I said the day before. I must have convinced her that I had more in the tank than I did. I smiled and put the envelope in my pocket.

"Did she say anything to you?" I asked the guy behind the counter.

"Nope," he said. "She just came in, canceled her membership, and told me to give that to you."

I couldn't believe it. I beat her. I actually beat her. I knew I could do it. "Well, I think I'm going to cancel my membership as well," I told the guy behind the counter. And that was it. That was the last time that any of us worked out with the Diesel.

The victory was bittersweet for me. On the one hand, I never *actually* quit. I *did* win fair and square. But I was so close to quitting; and *that's* what bothered me. If she had lasted one more day, I would have lost. I didn't know what to do with that.

***

I didn't see Jen for almost a year. I was at a coffee shop when she came in to grab a drink. I was taken back when I saw her. She looked great. That look of sad longing was gone from her eyes, and she had this glow to her. I never realized how beautiful she was.

I watched her as she waited in line, and I thought about what I should say to her. I looked at my reflection in the coffee shop window. I hadn't been back to the gym since the contest ended. The love handles were back, and my clothes weren't fitting the way they used to. I noticed a stain on my shirt. I realized I needed a haircut.

Oh well, I wasn't as easy on the eyes as I was a year ago, but I needed to go say, "hi." We never really had closure.

I waited until she ordered her drink and then I got up and made my way over to her. "Jen?" I asked cautiously.

She turned, and her eyes brightened when she saw me. "Michael!" She hugged me. "How have you been?"

"Pretty good," I said. "You?"

"I'm doing great," she said with a huge smile.

"You look great," I said, pointing out the obvious.

"Oh thanks." She blushed. "The D-3X has been good to me."

"You're still doing the program?" I asked, amazed.

"Yeah," she said. "It's been eighteen months. I feel like a new person compared to last year."

"Wow," was all I could say.

"You look good, too," she said, being kind.

I looked down and I noticed a ring on her finger. I motioned toward it. "Is that a..."

She looked down and then held out her hand. "Oh yeah. I met an amazing guy at my new job. He proposed last month and we're getting married in June!"

"Wow. Congratulations," I said. For some reason, I was sad to hear that she was getting married.

"You'll come to the wedding, right?" she asked.

"Of course."

"Great. I will send an invitation to the office so Kurt and Daphne can join us. It will be so great to have you guys there for my wedding. Listen, Michael, I never got a chance to thank you."

"What do you mean?" I asked.

"Well, the whole contest thing. That was a dark time in my life. I knew that I needed to make some changes, and I just didn't have it in me to make them by myself. The contest was what I needed to get my life back together. I am much happier now, and I couldn't have done it without you. Not to mention the Diesel!" She laughed as she said this last statement.

"Pain is weakness leaving the body," I said. She laughed again.

"I have to ask," I added. "How do you find the time to work out? I mean, life is so busy."

"Well," she said, "it's a priority to me. I'm a different person when I'm taking care of myself. I'm healthier. I'm happier. I'm... me. The Diesel is right. It's about change. It's about being the person you want to be. There are so many distractions out there. I have to remind myself what is really important. I have to remind myself of the person I want to be."

"Wow. That's really neat," I replied. I didn't know what else to say.

"It was nice running into you," she said. "I have to go, but I will send that invitation to the office."

"Great," I said. "I'm looking forward to it."

"It was really good to see you," she said, touching my arm. She hugged me, and then turned and walked out the door.

And with that, she was gone again.

I went back to my seat and thought about what just happened. She looked great. And she was happy. Why wasn't I happy? And why wasn't I happy for her? I couldn't believe she was still sticking to the D-3X program. How did she have the time? She must be obsessed. Maybe Jen wasn't as healthy as she seemed. Maybe she had issues. Who had time to commit to such a strict program? There were so many other worries in life. As I was thinking about what kind of disorder Jen must suffer from, my cell phone alerted me to an incoming text message. It was Chris. Oh no! I was late to our poker game! I packed up my stuff and hurried out the door.

"That same day Jesus went out of the house and sat beside the sea. And great crowds gathered about him, so that he got into a boat and sat down. And the whole crowd stood on the beach. And he told them many things in parables, saying: 'A sower went out to sow. And as he sowed, some seeds fell along the path, and the birds came and devoured them. Other seeds fell on rocky ground, where they did not have much soil, and immediately they sprang up, since they had no depth of soil, but when the sun rose they were scorched. And since they had no root, they withered away. Other seeds fell among thorns, and the thorns grew up and choked them. Other seeds fell on good soil and produced grain, some a hundredfold, some sixty, some thirty. He who has ears, let him hear.'" (Matthew 13:1–9)

MY FAVORITE BIBLE VERSE is John 6:68 (I know; it's weird). Jesus has just finished feeding a multitude, and then he launches into an esoteric message about the necessity of eating his flesh and drinking his blood. People are grossed out. With thousands of years of church liturgy in the rear-view mirror, this idea isn't *too* shocking to us, but to his original audience, it was outrageous. John tells us that many of Jesus's followers quit at these words.

Jesus, seeing the crowds thin, turns to the Twelve and asks, "Are you leaving, too?" Peter (as always) speaks for the Twelve and asks Jesus in John 6:68, "Where are we going to go? You have the words of eternal life." I have asked myself that same question many times in life. *Where else would I go? Jesus is life.*

The kingdom of God is about fidelity. Some call it "faith in Christ." Others call it "allegiance to Christ." My mother used to always tell me, "Keep the faith."

Jesus compared the kingdom to a sower and seed. A guy walks along and casts out some seed (a metaphor for the gospel message). Some falls on the path and is eaten by birds (a metaphor for people who hear the message and reject it immediately). Some falls on the rocky ground but is scorched by the sun (a metaphor for people who find the message compelling, but who fall away in suffering). Some falls among the thorns, where it is choked out by other plants (a metaphor for people who find the gospel beautiful, but value the things of the world more). Finally, there is the seed that falls on the good soil and bears fruit.

I wanted to do something different with this story—I wanted to tell it from the perspective of someone whose judgments about life were mostly wrong. While it's Michael's voice we hear throughout the narrative, Jen's actions represent the path of wisdom. Michael's thoughts and actions are sometimes erroneous and other times even toxic. While Diesel plays the role of Jesus in the story, he is a caricature of an extreme personal trainer, and his voice does not represent the words of God.

I am competitive. I also have spells where I am absolutely committed to health and fitness (I wish these spells were more consistent!). When I was doing my doctoral work, I put on some extra weight. When I graduated, I did not feel good about myself and decided it was time to get serious about my health. Some friends invited me to be a part of a health and fitness challenge in which we competed to see who could be the most consistent with exercise and healthy eating. They caught me at the wrong time because I was *absolutely* committed and I crushed it.

Most of the time, however, I am like Michael in my story—committed for a time but then back to unhealthy habits once I hit my fitness goal. The "thorns" of sleeping in and eating carbs choke out my motivation.

Most discussions on the parable of the sower devolve into arguments about whether the middle two soils are truly "saved." I will defer that question to people smarter than I am. Ultimately, our hope is placed in the mercy of God and the cross of Christ, not what kind of soil we are. The point of the parable is not: *What is the bare minimum of faith necessary to squeak into the kingdom?* The point of the parable is: *Satan, persecution, and riches will distract you from Jesus; stay the course!* "Keep the faith," as my mother would have told me.

When I was in my early twenties, I was trying to find my place in the world and in the church. I was a part of a church group for young adults, and I remember clearly one evening worship service we had in which I caught a glimpse of the glory of God. I don't know what it was, but I sensed God's presence and felt a vivid sense of *this is the kingdom of God.*

I wish I could say that every day with God is like that. They aren't. I have had other moments in life in which I caught glimpses of God—in worship services, at the birth of a child, on a mountain vista, but most of the time, life with God is about persevering. It's about keeping the faith. It's about awaiting our redemption.

Jesus tells us, "The thief comes only to steal and kill and destroy. I came that they may have life and have it abundantly."[1] Jesus is life. Following him is the narrow way. It's difficult and full of distractions. There will be times of ecstasy. There will be times of pain and grief. There will be times when you want to walk away.

But where are you going to go? Jesus has the words of eternal life. Keep the faith.

QUESTIONS FOR REFLECTION

1. Have you ever had to persevere through something hard? What was it and what did that time feel like?

2. If you were one of Jesus's disciples hearing this parable for the first time, what would you think about the soils?

3. For the soil landing on the path, Jesus says that Satan immediately takes away the word. What are some ways you have seen Satan turn people away from the gospel?

4. What is a bigger distraction for you: hardship or the lure of riches?

5. Jesus says that the gospel bears fruit in the good soil. What are some of the ways God has breathed life into you?

6. Is there someone in your life who can encourage you when life is hard? Who would that be?

1. John 10:10.

Trouble

"Religion that is pure and undefiled before God the Father is this: to visit orphans and widows in their affliction, and to keep oneself unstained from the world." (James 1:27)

HAVE YOU EVER BEEN in trouble? Have you ever been trapped? Have you ever done something so bad, so unthinkable, that you thought your life was over? As much as it hurts to be lonely, scared, or unsure, nothing is worse than being alone and in trouble. Last year, I was in trouble.

No one would have expected *me* to get in trouble. I was always the good girl, the responsible one, the last girl anyone would expect to do something wrong. But last year, I did something foolish and ended up in trouble.

You see, there was this guy, Tyler McKinney. He was faultless—captivating blue eyes, thick, flowing brown hair, and a smile that could light up a room. He was captain of the lacrosse team, runner-up for homecoming king, and, what's more, he liked me—and I liked him back. Like I said, he was perfect—except for one small thing—Tyler was not a Christian. Our youth pastor Mike told us that God doesn't want us to date non-Christians because we're not yoked the same, or something like that. I didn't understand what God had against Tyler or how his not going to church meant we weren't yoked the same. It's not like he was a Satanist or anything. Why wouldn't God want me to date the boy of my dreams? I wasn't going to *marry* him. God wants me to be happy, doesn't he?

People say that opposites attract, and this was certainly the case with Tyler and me. Tyler was more of a free spirit, and well, he had a reputation. Most of it was untrue, but enough of it *was* true that you might call him a rebel.

So, when Tyler invited me to a party at his older brother's fraternity, I was torn. The old me said that I didn't want to make God mad. But another part of me said that Tyler was The One and that God would understand. Maybe I needed to learn how to take more risks. Maybe I needed to loosen up. Maybe I could even be a positive influence in Tyler's life. Maybe God wanted to use me to reach Tyler. He did stuff like that didn't he?

I told my friends Liz, Erin, and Jess about Tyler and the party, thinking that they would be excited for me. I was wrong. There was a reason why the old me was friends with these girls. They reminded me what Pastor Mike said about not being yoked the same. How could I want to date someone who wasn't a Christian?

They were just jealous. Jess had a secret crush on Tyler since first grade, and it killed her that he would like me. Liz hadn't been on a date in her whole life and didn't want *me* to have a boyfriend. And Erin? Well, sometimes she was just mean.

Against my friends' advice, I decided to go to the party. I lied to my parents and told them I was staying at Liz's house. Tyler picked me up at school so they wouldn't get suspicious. I was so nervous. I had never done anything like this before. I was always good little Allie, always in church, always doing the right thing. But that Allie wasn't going to end up with Tyler McKinney. New Allie was.

Tyler showed up in his '05 Boxter and took me to his brother's fraternity about an hour away. When we got to the house I was hit with a cascade of new sights, sounds, and smells. The music was so loud I could feel it; people were moving to the energy of the music—some rhythmically, some not—and there was beer everywhere. In fact, the whole place reeked of it. We walked through the front room toward the kitchen. On the way, I noticed a couple on the couch. She looked pale and nauseated. He was laughing hysterically at a joke that apparently no one else got.

When we got to the kitchen, someone from the back yelled, "Oh man, who let *him* in here?" It was Tyler's brother. Tyler went over and faked a punch to his brother's stomach. The two then locked hands and slapped each other on the back. Tyler's brother graduated the year before. He had been quite the partier in high school and apparently hadn't changed much in college.

Someone handed Tyler a drink, which he immediately passed to me. I smiled nervously and thanked him. Was I really going to do this? Was this really who I was? The old Allie never would have found herself in this situation. But the old Allie was gone. I took a drink.

I masked my disgust as I swallowed the bitter drink. Did people actually like this stuff? How could they? It tasted like carbonated pee, only worse. I finished the drink and was promptly handed another one.

"Let's dance!" Tyler said, grabbing my hand and taking me into the other room.

The rest of the evening is a little blurry to me now. I know we danced. I know we drank. I know he kissed me. But the rest I don't remember. That's why I say I was in trouble.

I woke up the next morning still dressed from the previous night. I couldn't remember going to bed or even coming home. Everything was a blur. My head was killing me and I felt sick to my stomach. Why is it again that people drink?

In addition to the headaches and nausea, something else wasn't right. I didn't feel right... down there. I was sore, like cramping, only worse. I had never hurt like that before. Why would I hurt like that unless... did Tyler and I...? How could we? I didn't remember a thing.

The nausea started to overwhelm me, and I stumbled toward the bathroom. I puked my guts out and then collapsed on the cold tile floor. I could smell vomit in my hair as I tried to remember what happened. My mind was racing. Did we or didn't we? What if we did? What if it wasn't him? Was I raped? What if I am pregnant... or worse? My stomach started churning again at this last thought. I propped myself up again and dry-heaved over the toilet.

I sat there, staring at my reflection in the bowl and I wondered what had happened to me. What did I do? Who did I do it with? What's going to happen to me? What do I do *now*? I need to talk to someone. But who do I talk to? I couldn't tell my parents. They would freak. I didn't want to disappoint them. They were so proud of what a "fine young woman I am turning into," and I didn't want to wreck that. I couldn't tell Liz, or Erin, or Jess. They *told* me not to go to the party. But who could I tell? Who could I trust? Pastor Mike?

***

The next day I was sitting outside of Pastor Mike's office, waiting for him to finish a phone call. The church foyer felt sterile, like the waiting room at a doctor's office. I could hear Mike chatting on the phone down the hall. He was talking to someone about driving or chaperoning or something like that. It was tough to tell from where I was. I sat there outside his office looking at pictures on the wall and trying to think about what I was going to say to him.

There was this picture on the wall of this young guy wearing jeans and a T-shirt. He looked like he was about to collapse from exhaustion, but he was being propped up by Jesus from behind. In his hands were a hammer and a nail. The picture was all dark except for the beams of light emanating from Jesus.

I sat there, looking at the picture, puzzled. I think I understood it. The guy was ready to give up, but Jesus was sustaining him. I'd like to think that was true. But the picture seemed out of place in the church foyer—almost like a cute picture of kittens hanging on the wall at a dentist's office. No one thinks about kittens while they wait for a root canal. I sat there looking at this picture and I felt like I should be comforted by it, but I wasn't.

While I was looking at the picture of Jesus and the guy with the hammer, Mike finished his conversation and came out to see me. "Allie," he said with a smile, "Sorry to keep you waiting. How's it going?"

"Pretty good," I said reservedly.

Mike held the door open and motioned for me to come into his office. I went in and found a seat as he closed the door behind us. "So, what's up?" he asked.

"Well, I wanted to talk to you. I have... this... friend. I'm worried about her. She's been, like, going to parties and stuff, and I think she's drinking."

Mike leaned forward in his seat. "Really? That's pretty risky. I'd be worried about your friend, too. Teenagers can do stupid things when they're drinking." He furrowed his brow as he talked, like he was trying to read my mind. His tone was stern, like a parent talking to a child who just pulled his sister's hair. "Tell me, do your friend's parents know what she's doing?"

I froze. Why did he ask *that*? "No. She can't tell them because they wouldn't understand. They're, like, really strict, and she doesn't want to get into trouble." I fidgeted in my chair as I went on about my "friend," hoping he wouldn't catch on that I was talking about myself. What if he told my parents? They would freak. They might kick me out. Then what would I do?

"You know, Allie. You should confront your friend. The Bible tells us that we shouldn't be drunk on wine, but filled with the Spirit." There was an air of triumph in his voice, like an athlete responding to a reporter about how hard he trained to win a championship. He quoted Scripture like it was a workout routine. Do this and you win; don't and you're a loser. I don't know why, but his very mention of the Bible made me want to crawl under my chair and hide. My thoughts went to the picture of Jesus in the waiting room. "In fact," Mike continued, "maybe you shouldn't be spending so much time with this friend. She sounds like a bad girl. Her behavior is taking her somewhere you don't want to go. She could get pregnant. Then what would she do? Her life would be over."

I sat there, horrified. Did he know? Did someone tell him? Maybe he could see it on my face. Suddenly I needed to get out of there. I had made a mistake in coming to Pastor Mike. I couldn't tell him what I did. My stomach churned as I remembered my situation. I was trapped. My mind raced through worst-case scenarios as Mike rambled about the dangers of teenage drinking. All I could think about was how I could have been so stupid.

"Allie, are you okay?" Mike interrupted. "You look like you might be sick."

"Yeah, I'm okay. I think it's something I ate."

"Allie, we should pray for your friend. I am worried about her and I don't want her to get into trouble. I think you should confront her or tell her parents what is going on. What's your friend's name?"

I panicked. I hadn't thought about that. I blurted out the first name that came to my mind. "Liz," I said.

"Liz from youth group?" Mike said, astonished.

"No, not that Liz," I backtracked. Of all the names I could have made up... "Another Liz... from school. She doesn't go to church here." I felt like an idiot. He was never going to buy this.

But he did buy it. We bowed our heads and we prayed for Liz. I prayed that God would speak to Liz, that she would realize how foolish she was being and that she would stop going to parties. I also prayed that God would not let Liz get pregnant.

So that was it. I tried going to Pastor Mike, but he wasn't able to help me. But I didn't know who else to talk to. My parents would freak, and my friends would just say, "I told you so." So I kept it to myself. I pretended nothing was wrong. My parents never asked questions and they didn't suspect anything.

But the secret was eating me up. I couldn't concentrate at school. I couldn't focus on my homework. I stopped going to youth group. I didn't really even want to get out of bed in the morning.

What's worse is that Tyler was avoiding me. He wouldn't answer my calls, and he was evading me at school. He was either equally upset over whatever happened that night, or he was a total jerk. Either way, he wasn't going to help me. I was in trouble, I was trapped, and I couldn't talk to anyone about it.

Or so I thought.

***

Four weeks after the party, I got into it with my friends at lunch. We were sitting in the cafeteria at our usual table. Liz was complaining about Becky Jennings, another girl at school. Becky was the head cheerleader and all the guys were in love with her. I was kind of half-listening as I ate my yogurt. Thoughts of pregnancy and STDs made Liz's gripes seem pretty petty.

"Did you see what Becky was wearing the other day?" Liz asked indignantly. "I can't believe she left the house in a skirt that short. What a slut."

My ears perked up as I heard that word. "You shouldn't call people that," I interrupted.

She stopped and scowled at me. "I'm not the only one who thinks she's a slut. Everyone knows it." She folded her arms smugly.

"I'm just saying," I said. "You never know why people do what they do, so maybe you shouldn't be so quick to judge."

Liz huffed. "What's your problem, anyway, Allie? You've been acting really weird lately, and you haven't been to church in like a month."

I sat there silent as my friends stared at me, waiting for an answer. I sensed my chance to come clean. Was I really going to do this? Was I going to tell them? They weren't always the most sympathetic girls, but they were my friends. Maybe they would understand that I made a mistake. Maybe they could help me.

"Well..." I started. I decided I would risk letting them know what was bothering me. After all, the secret was eating me up and I didn't know who else I could tell. "Remember when I told you about that party Tyler invited me to?"

"Oh my gosh, Allie. You didn't actually go, did you?" Liz looked at me with a mix of horror and contempt.

"Yeah, I did."

"How could you?" said Erin. "You know God doesn't want you to date Tyler McKinney. He's not a Christian."

"I know he doesn't go to church, but it's not like he's a Satanist or anything. I thought maybe I could be a good influence on him."

"Wasn't the party supposed to be at a fraternity?" Jess said. "How were you going to be a good influence on him there?"

I was speechless.

"Did you drink alcohol?" Liz sneered.

Again, I was speechless.

"Oh my gosh, you did." Erin said.

My friends were all glaring at me like I was on trial. I knew it was a mistake to tell them. They couldn't know everything that happened. They'd freak. They'd tell the whole school. They'd tell my parents. I needed to get out of there, and quick.

"Allie, I thought you were a Christian," Jess said.

"Excuse me. I have to go." I got up from the table and hurried out in to the hallway toward my locker. My friends sat there, stunned, as I left. This was a disaster. How did I get myself into this situation? I thought I was a

Christian. But stuff like this doesn't happen to Christians. Christians do the right thing. They make good choices. Maybe Liz was right about Becky, and maybe she was right about me.

***

I found my locker and fumbled with the lock as I tried to remember the combination. My mind was filled with thoughts of pregnancy and disease. What was I going to do? Who could I talk to? Was there anyone who would listen? I laid my head down against my locker and my eyes started to tear.

"Well, if it isn't the Virgin Mary." I looked up and saw Gus Romero walking down the deserted hallway toward me. "Any Jesus sightings?"

Gus was so gross. He was wearing leather pants and a tight tee shirt. He was outspokenly gay, he hated Christians, and he always gave us a hard time for our faith.

"Go away, Gus." I said. "You know, you shouldn't make fun of God like that. One day you're going to have to stand before him."

"Oooh I'm scared."

I was too tired to deal with Gus right then. I looked back down at my locker and continued to fumble with the combination, but I was too distracted to get it open. My eyes were tearing and I couldn't contain a short sob.

"Are you crying?" Gus asked with amusement.

I turned to him and shouted, "I told you to go away, Gus! Leave me alone!"

Gus's countenance changed when I yelled at him. He went from haughty aggression to what looked like genuine concern. "Are you okay? Really?" he asked. "Why are you crying?"

"Don't you have a parade to go to or something? Why don't you give someone else a hard time?" I really was not in the mood to be chided. I just wanted to hide somewhere and be by myself. But Gus wouldn't go away.

"Allie," he said with an air of compassion. "You don't look good at all. What happened?"

My face was still buried in my locker. I was a mess. My face was flushed and my makeup ran everywhere. I whimpered as I tried to hold back the sobs. Why did I have to be alone right now? Why, when I needed them the most, were my friends so cold? My mind went back to the picture of Jesus in the waiting room at the church. Where was he? We talk about Jesus being a comforter and a friend to the friendless. Was any of that true? I sure wasn't seeing that from his people.

I looked up at Gus to beg him one more time to go away, but I was taken aback at what I saw. His attention was fixed on me and there was a look of concern on his eyes that made him seem unusually... human. For the first time, he looked like a person, not a gay person.

The flood of emotions must have been too much for me, because I started to faint. Gus caught me as I fell forward and he propped me up as I regained my strength. "Allie," he asked again. "What's going on?"

A few minutes ago, Gus grossed me out more than any other guy at school, but now with him I felt safe to talk for the first time.

"Do you know Tyler McKinney?" I began. I don't know if it was the adrenaline rush from almost fainting, or the relief of finally uncorking what was bottled inside, but I spilled everything to him—the party, the drinking, the lies, *everything*.

"I don't know what happened that night, but I must have passed out and... I think I was raped." With this last confession I could no longer withhold the tears. I fell forward on his shoulder and started sobbing. He stood there with me, holding me as I cried and he didn't say a word. When he finally did speak, all he said was, "It's not your fault, Allie," and then, "It's going to be okay."

We stood there in the empty hallway for what seemed an eternity before he spoke again. "You know," he said, "there is a clinic in town where you can go to find out if you're pregnant. I can go with you if you want." I pulled away from his shoulder and looked in his eyes. "Why?" I asked. "Why are you being nice to me?"

I had always been mean to Gus. He was mean to me. But now he was... different. I couldn't tell why.

He seemed to be holding back his own tears as he said to me, "I know what it's like to have secrets."

It's been said that the most comforting words in the English language are, "me too." That's what I needed to hear. Maybe Gus was right. Maybe it *was* going to be okay. Maybe my parents *weren't* going to freak. I started to think about how I would tell them, and a weight began to lift off my shoulders. Maybe I *could* get through this. Maybe the old me wasn't gone after all. A smile began to spread across my face as I hugged Gus again. It was going to be okay.

"And behold, a lawyer stood up to put him to the test, saying, 'Teacher, what shall I do to inherit eternal life?' He said to him, 'What is written in the Law? How do you read it?' And he answered, 'You shall love the Lord your God with all your heart and with all your soul and with all your strength and with all your mind, and your neighbor as yourself.' And he said to him, 'You have answered correctly; do this, and you will live.' But he, desiring to justify himself, said to Jesus, 'And who is my neighbor?' Jesus replied, 'A man was going down from Jerusalem to Jericho, and he fell among robbers, who stripped him and beat him and departed, leaving him half dead. Now by chance a priest was going down that road, and when he saw him he passed by on the other side. So likewise a Levite, when he came to the place and saw him, passed by on the other side. But a Samaritan, as he journeyed, came to where he was, and when he saw him, he had compassion. He went to him and bound up his wounds, pouring on oil and wine. Then he set him on his own animal and brought him to an inn and took care of him. And the next day he took out two denarii and gave them to the innkeeper, saying, "Take care of him, and whatever more you spend, I will repay you when I come back." Which of these three, do you think, proved to be a neighbor to the man who fell among the robbers?' He said, 'The one who showed him mercy.' And Jesus said to him, 'You go, and do likewise.'" (Luke 10:25–37)

I'M GLAD YOU'RE STILL reading.

There is a reason I saved this parable for near the end. If it offended you, or if you think I have mischaracterized or misrepresented any of the characters in the story, then I have done a pretty good job of modernizing this parable that Jesus told 2,000 years ago. When Jesus originally told this parable, it was provocative. It was offensive. It has become tame to us (it's one of the first Bible stories we tell our kids), but to the original audience it was *shocking*.

The big disconnect between us and the original hearers of this parable is the connotation of the word "Samaritan." When we hear that word, we naturally think "good Samaritan." It's literally the only context in which we use the word. We know the story too well: A Samaritan is a person who helps someone in need.

That is not what the ancient Israelites would have thought about Samaritans. The Gospel of John tells us that in the ancient world, "Jews have no dealings with Samaritans."[1] If you asked the original audience to blurt out the first word that came to mind when they heard the word "Samaritan," they would not have said "good," they would have said something like "pagan," "idolater," "half-breed," or "dog."

They didn't like Samaritans.

After the priest and the Levite pass by the man without helping, the turn in the story happens when a Samaritan becomes the unlikely hero. Priests and Levites were praised for their religious devotion, but in Jesus' story, it is the Samaritan who acts like a neighbor to the man in trouble.

Religious devotion does not preclude compassion. The priest and the Levite were probably not heartless. They didn't pass by on the other side of the road because they were appalled at having to be inconvenienced by helping someone. They passed by on the other side because they thought the guy was dead and they didn't want to defile themselves.

The Law of Moses prohibited people from serving in the temple when they were unclean from touching dead things. If the priest or the Levite had touched the man's corpse, they would have been disqualified for ministry. And Jesus's message in this story was that these guys missed the point. They came across someone in trouble, and all they could think about was, "If that guy is dead and I touch him, I can't do the work of the ministry." They missed the point.

In the same way, the pastor and the Christian friends in my story missed the point. The road from Jerusalem to Jericho was hazardous, and the man in Jesus' story made a mistake traveling it by himself. The original hearers may have thought things like, "he shouldn't have traveled that road by himself." Similarly, the religious characters in my story pointed out mistakes that Allie made. They even quoted Bible verses to her. None of that is necessarily a bad thing, but it wasn't what she needed. What she needed was compassion, and she got it from an unlikely source.

Even our enemies are our neighbors.

The question that leads into the parable is not "How should I live?" or "What does it mean to be a Christian?" The question asked of Jesus was,

1. John 4:9.

"Who is my neighbor?" The parable addresses the question of who it is we have a responsibility to love. Jesus's answer is that even your enemy is your neighbor. Even the people who don't look like you. Even the people who don't worship the same God as you. Even the people who don't live the same way you do. Even your enemy is your neighbor.

When I was in seminary, I waited tables to pay my bills. I worked in downtown Dallas and rubbed shoulders with many different walks of life among the working poor. One of my coworkers was a guy named Fidel.

He was awful to me.

Fidel lost a loved one tragically at a young age and subsequently carried around a lot of anger toward God. My being a seminary student triggered these emotions in him and he took every opportunity to bully me. He was critical, mocking, and belittling. I spent a lot of time in prayer over my relationship to Fidel, not knowing what to do about this coworker who was so hostile to me.

Then one day, he changed. He smiled at me more. He helped me. He was kind. The turnaround was so obvious that I had to ask him what happened. It was the first time I braved bringing up a personal question with him, and when I asked, he just smiled and pointed one finger up toward the sky.

Later, he and I shared a meal together and he told me his story. He told me about his loss and his anger toward God. He told me how I triggered that anger. And then he told me about what had happened to him that week. He was driving around downtown and he just felt God telling him to go to church. He hadn't been to church in decades, but he found one, went inside and prayed. Someone at the church shared the gospel with him and he became a Christian. His life was one of the most radical turnarounds I have ever witnessed.

Fidel became a good friend—one of my best. We never know when our enemies will become brothers or sisters. But brother, sister, or enemy—they are always our neighbor.

QUESTIONS FOR REFLECTION

1. Have you ever been in trouble? What did it look like and who helped you?

2. What were your immediate reactions to *my* story? Did Jesus's parable have the same effect on you?

3. What are some ways that we let religious devotion prevent us from showing compassion?

4. Have you ever been treated like a Samaritan? What did that feel like?

5. Who are some people we treat as Samaritans today?

6. Who is God calling you to be a neighbor to today?

Sons

"Just so, I tell you, there will be more joy in heaven over one sinner who repents than over ninety-nine righteous persons who need no repentance." (Luke 15:7)

MARSHALL SAT IN SILENCE gazing at the artwork on the wall of his father's hospital room. The painting was a non-descript body of water with the Pacific Northwest mountains towering in the background. Orcas and salmon raced around in the water below.

How strange, Marshall thought. *I wonder who decorates these rooms and how they decide what to display—nice enough to look good but not so nice that someone would be tempted to steal it.*

The ticking of the clock and the occasional beep of the hospital machinery were the only sounds in the room. His dad, Ken, slept in the bed beside him, cancer having robbed him of his color and strength.

So, this is how it ends, Marshall thought. A beautiful life would conclude in an empty hospital room.

Tears began to form in his eyes as a knock sounded at the door.

"Hello?" the doctor's voice called as he entered.

"Yes, hi, come in." Marshall said.

The sound of the two men talking woke Marshall's father. The old man stirred and began to look around, confused.

"The doctor's here, Dad," Marshall said.

"How are you feeling, Mr. Caldwell?" the doctor said.

"Oh, I'm alive. That's something to be grateful for."

The doctor smiled and nodded. "Well, you have a great son to be here with you at the hospital."

"I have two great sons," Ken interrupted. "My younger son lives in Idaho. He couldn't be here."

Marshall clenched his teeth a little at the mention of Cameron. *Couldn't be here,* Marshall wondered to himself, *or* chose not *to be here?*

"You must be very proud," the doctor responded.

Ken smiled.

"Well, Mr. Caldwell," the doctor began, "unfortunately I come bearing bad news. The test results have come back, and it is as we suspected. There is nothing else we can do for you but keep you comfortable."

Ken smiled and nodded his head. "I know, I know, Doctor. It's my time. I can feel it. Thank you for all you have done for me."

Marshall's eyes began to tear again at his father's pain-free acceptance of the prognosis. Dad was ready to go, but was *he* ready to let him go?

Marshall's brain was in a fog as his father and the doctor talked options. Finally, the other two men shook hands and the doctor turned to leave. "I'm sorry," he said as he took the doorknob. "We'll take good care of you." And with that, he left.

"I'm so sorry, Dad—" Marshall began before his father cut him off.

"Marshall, it's okay. It's time. I'm ready. I've been ready for a while."

"I understand," Marshal said. "I just don't know if I'm ready."

"You're ready," his father said. "You're a good man—a good husband, a good father, and a good son. I couldn't have asked for anyone better to be with me at the end."

"I will bring Tracy and Codie by the day after tomorrow," Marshall assured his father. His wife and son suspected this was the end, but it would be tough for them to say goodbye, nonetheless.

"Thank you, Marshall. I hope you are as proud of your son as I am of you."

"I am," Marshall said through tears.

He reached out and grabbed his father's hand. Silence hung in the air. Marshall was again aware of the ticking clock and the beeping machines.

"Your brother called me yesterday," Ken finally said.

Marshall perked up, surprised. "W-What?"

"Yeah. I was just as surprised. I call him every Sunday. He never answers, but I always leave a voice mail telling him I love him. I never knew if he listened to them, but this last time I told him I was dying. He called me back yesterday."

Marshall's muscles tightened. "I don't know what to say," he said, shaking his head.

"He's coming back," Ken replied, choking back tears.

"I don't want to see him," Marshall interrupted. "After what he did to you and Mom, I don't *ever* want to see him."

"How long has it been?" Ken asked.

"Since Mom died. Five years. It can be forty-five more for all I care."

"Son, your brother's been gone for five years and he's coming back. I want you to call him."

"Dad, I can't—"

"Please," his father insisted. "It was just money. I forgave him a long time ago."

"It's not the money," Marshall said. "That was your *life*. You could have been much more comfortable in your old age."

"I never complained," Ken said. "Your brother made mistakes, but we all have our demons."

Marshall shook his head, searching for words. "I still can't believe he did it. I don't think I can ever forgive him."

"For me, the only thing left is to see the two of you reconciled. Please call him."

Marshall took a deep breath. "I don't know if I can, Dad. But I will pray about it."

"Please do," his dad said with a smile. "All is forgiven."

***

Marshall went home with a heavy heart. When he walked in the door, his wife Tracy was busy making dinner.

"Welcome home!" she called from the other room.

"Thank you," he responded sullenly.

Tracy came into the entryway to greet him. "How was it?"

"Hard."

"I am so sorry."

"The test results came back. It is as we expected. There is nothing else they can do for him."

Tracy pursed her lips and nodded. "I am *so* sorry," she repeated.

"He's taking it very well. I think he's ready to go. I just don't know if *I* am ready for him to go," Marshall said.

"I bet," Tracy said. "He's a good dad."

Marshall was silent for a moment. "He is a good dad. Better than Cam and I deserve."

Tracy nodded in understanding.

"He wants me to call Cam," Marshall continued.

Tracy nodded pensively. "Can you do that?"

"I don't know," Marshall said, choking back tears. "After what he did, I don't know if I can. I told him I would pray about it."

"That's good," Tracy said. "I know that would be hard for you, but I think it would mean the world to your dad."

"I know," Marshall said. "He said as much. I don't see how he got over everything so easily."

"He's a good man," Tracy said. "Well, I think you should give it some thought."

"Yeah."

"I don't want to pile on," Tracy said hesitantly, "but I had a rough day as well."

Marshall looked up. "Oh yeah?"

"Yeah. It's about Codie."

"Okay. Where is he?"

"He's at a friend's. He'll be back tonight. But I got a phone call from the Kellys today."

"The Kellys? What did they want with Codie? Did something happen with their dog?"

"No," Tracy said. "But it's related to that."

"Okay."

"When he dog sat for them, they gave him a house key."

"Right. I remember."

"Well, apparently, he made a copy of the key and earlier this week he broke into their house."

"What?!" Marshall said. "That can't be true."

"That's what I said," Tracy replied. "But apparently they have him on security video."

"They are sure it is him? What did he do?"

"They are pretty sure it's him. They said he stole a laptop and vandalized their house," Tracy said. "I'm just sick about the whole thing. And all of this on top of your dad, it's just awful."

"Yeah," Marshall said. "I can't believe it. Did they call the police? What is going to happen?"

"They didn't call the police," Tracy said a little more cheerfully. "They said they wanted to talk to us first."

"First?" Marshall asked. "Like they *are* going to call the police?"

"I don't know," Tracy said. "We didn't talk long. I couldn't handle it and I wanted to talk to you."

"OK," Marshall said. "I'll give them a call and maybe we can sort this out."

***

The next day, Marshall and Tracy found themselves seated in Travis and Courtney Kelly's living room, coffees in hand.

"I am so sorry to have to get together under these circumstances," Travis began. "I hope you know that we think the world of you, and we think Codie is a good kid. Teenagers just do things on impulse sometimes."

"So, tell us what happened," Marshall said.

"Well," Courtney said. "On Tuesday after work, I came home to a mess that wasn't there when I left in the morning. Papers and books were on the floor, a lamp was knocked over—it looked like someone just ran wild in the place. Then I saw the damage to the piano, and I knew someone had been in here. I didn't know if they were still here or what, so I ran outside and called Travis."

"I have the cameras linked to an app," Travis said. "We live in such a quiet neighborhood that I turn the notifications off, but I was able to pull up the footage right away. Here is what I saw." He handed his phone to Marshall, who huddled up with Tracy to watch the footage.

Sure enough, it was unmistakable. The person in the video was Codie. Tracy gasped. Marshall gave the phone back to Travis—he couldn't watch the rest.

"So, what were the damages?" Marshall asked.

Travis and Courtney looked at each other. "The damage to the piano alone is thousands," began Courtney. "Plus there is the missing laptop. . ."

"How much?" Marshall interrupted.

Silence hung in the air.

Travis finally spoke up. "We don't know for sure, but we suspect the damage is close to $10,000."

Tears began to form in Marshall's eyes. Tracy buried her face in her hands. "OK," Marshall said. "We will cover it all. When you know the exact amount, just let me know. We will pay it. No questions asked. Let's just keep the police out of this."

Visions of his son in court began to flood Marshall's mind. He would have a criminal record. What would happen next? What if this was just the tip of the iceberg? Would he graduate? Could he go to college? Would there be more trouble? What if this was just the first step in a downward spiral?

Travis and Courtney looked at each other again. This time it was Travis who spoke up. "Do you really think it's best to keep the police out of it? I mean, I don't know what he's going through right now. I know your dad is sick. But do you think there would be some value to letting him experience some consequences?"

Already fighting tears, Marshall's mind went back to his son in court. "No, I am sure," Marshall said adamantly. "I will take care of this. Just tell me the amount and I will pay it."

The Kellys were silent.

"I just don't know—" Travis began.

"Travis," Marshall interrupted, "this is my *son*. I don't want to lose him."

Courtney and Travis looked at each other in sadness and sympathy. "OK," Travis finally said. "We will keep this between ourselves."

Relief flushed through Marshall's body as the image of his son in court vanished. He had him back.

***

The next day, Marshall, Tracy, and Codie stood in Ken's hospital room to reminisce and say goodbye.

"Remember when Codie was little," Tracy said, "and you used to walk him past the construction sites every day?"

Ken laughed. "He knew the names of every truck at that site. He would have sat there for hours watching them if we let him."

Even the teenager smiled at that.

"Thanks for everything, Grandpa," Codie said. "I'm going to miss you."

"You've brought me true joy," Ken said. "I am so proud of the man you are becoming."

Codie looked at the ground, fighting back tears.

"Codie, let's give your dad a minute," Tracy said. She and her son left the hospital room, closing the door behind them.

"He's a good kid," Ken said to his son. "He's going to be okay. This thing with the house—it will all blow over."

"I know," Marshall said, getting emotional. "But I worry about him so much. I thought we had lost him, Dad. Our neighbors had every right to prosecute him. They probably *should* have. We're making him do 200 hours of community service at the food bank to pay us back, but for a moment, I thought he was gone for good."

"I know what you are going through," Ken said, taking his son's hand. "I wish I could tell you it gets easier. I can't. But I *can* tell you it will be okay."

"Did I give you this much trouble?" Marshall asked, smiling now.

Ken laughed deeply. "No, not you. I never worried about you. I always knew where you were and when you were coming home. You were always with me. Your brother, on the other hand, I lost a lot of sleep worrying about him."

Marshall's countenance fell at the mention of Cam. Silence filled the room.

"Have you thought about calling him?" Ken finally asked.

Marshall shook his head vigorously as he searched for the words. "I can't, Dad. After everything he did to you, to Mom, to me."

"To you?" Ken asked.

"Dad, where is he? If this were the first time he was absent, that would be one thing, but he's been gone for years. Everything has fallen on *me*—arrangements for Mom, the house, your care, even now at the end. It's *all* on me. He doesn't care about anyone but himself."

"Son, these last years since your mom died have been my favorite years with you. You've been with me through everything. You know, when you were a boy, we never worried about you. We always knew you'd be okay. But Cam . . . we thought we would lose him. We spent *so* much time trying to save him. My whole life I had regrets—that maybe I worried too much about Cam and neglected *you*. But in these last years, watching you care for your mother and then for me—I am amazed at the man you have become."

"Thank you," Marshall said, holding back tears.

"He needs you, Marshall. When I am gone, you're all he'll have."

"I can't, Dad. I can't forgive him."

"You forgave Codie."

"He's a boy. Cam is a grown man."

"He'll always be your boy, Marshall. No matter how old you get. Where could he go where you wouldn't chase him?"

"Nowhere," Marshall said.

"What could he do that you wouldn't forgive?"

"Nothing," Marshall replied. "He's my son."

"Cam is *my* son," Ken said. "And *your* brother. Call him. If you can't do this for you, then do it for me."

A few moments later, Marshall rejoined his wife and son in the hallway.

"How is he holding up?" Tracy asked.

"He's good, as always," Marshall responded.

"Are you ready to go?" Tracy asked.

"You two go ahead," Marshall replied. "I have a phone call to make."

"And he said, 'There was a man who had two sons. And the younger of them said to his father, "Father, give me the share of property that is coming to me." And he divided his property between them. Not many days later, the younger son gathered all he had and took a journey into a far country, and there he squandered his property in reckless living. And when he had spent everything, a severe famine arose in that country, and he began to be in need. So he went and hired himself out to one of the citizens of that country, who sent him into his fields to feed pigs. And he was longing to be fed with the pods that the pigs ate, and no one gave him anything.

'But when he came to himself, he said, "How many of my father's hired servants have more than enough bread, but I perish here with hunger! I will arise and go to my father, and I will say to him, 'Father, I have sinned against heaven and before you. I am no longer worthy to be called your son. Treat me as one of your hired servants.'" And he arose and came to his father. But while he was still a long way off, his father saw him and felt compassion, and ran and embraced him and kissed him. And the son said to him, "Father, I have sinned against heaven and before you. I am no longer worthy to be called your son." But the father said to his servants, "Bring quickly the best robe, and put it on him, and put a ring on his hand, and shoes on his feet. And bring the fattened calf and kill it, and let us eat and celebrate. For this my son was dead, and is alive again; he was lost, and is found."

And they began to celebrate.

'Now his older son was in the field, and as he came and drew near to the house, he heard music and dancing. And he called one of the servants and asked what these things meant. And he said to him, "Your brother has come, and your father has killed the fattened calf, because he has received him back safe and sound." But he was angry and refused to go in. His father came out and entreated him, but he answered his father, "Look, these many years I have served you, and I never disobeyed your command, yet you never gave me a young goat, that I might

celebrate with my friends. But when this son of yours came,
who has devoured your property with prostitutes, you killed the
fattened calf for him!" And he said to him, "Son, you are always
with me, and all that is mine is yours. It was fitting to celebrate
and be glad, for this your brother was dead, and is alive; he was
lost, and is found."" (Luke 15:11–32)

THE PARABLE OF THE Prodigal Son or the Parable of the Lost Son, or, as I like to call it, "The Parable of the Lost Son*s*" is probably the greatest story ever told. It's been called the gospel *within* the gospel. It is absolutely brilliant and impossible to duplicate.

One of the things that makes Jesus' story so brilliant is that even though it has one main point, it also makes a million other beautiful points. I couldn't capture them all, so I focused on the main point of the parable, which we are told in Luke 15:1–2: "Now the tax collectors and sinners were all drawing near to hear him. And the Pharisees and the scribes grumbled, saying, 'This man receives sinners and eats with them.'"[1]

Jesus received sinners and the Pharisees grumbled about it. In response, Jesus tells three stories in rapid succession—the parable of the lost sheep, the parable of the lost coin, and the parable of the lost son.

In the parable of the lost sheep, a man has one hundred sheep, loses one, finds it and then rejoices. Jesus says, "Just so, I tell you, there will be more joy in heaven over one sinner who repents than over ninety-nine righteous persons who need no repentance."[2]

Then, he launches right into the parable of the lost coin, where a woman has ten coins, loses one, searches and finds it, and then rejoices. It has pretty much the same plotline as the parable of the lost sheep. Likewise, the parable of the lost son has the same plotline.

Why did Jesus tell the same story three times?

They escalate in intensity and build up to the story of the older brother.

In agrarian societies, wealth can be measured in livestock. In the first parable, the man with the 100 sheep loses 1 percent of them, therefore a guy loses 1 percent of his 401K. In the second parable, the coin that the woman loses is probably part of her dowry—it could have been the equivalent of an

1. Luke 15:1–2.
2. Luke 15:7.

engagement ring. (Now you understand why she tore the house up looking for it.)

So, the stories have gone from losing 1 percent of a 401K to 10 percent of an engagement ring. The stakes are higher! In the third story, a man loses one of his two children. It's the ultimate story of loss and finding.

Jesus' story can be divided into two halves. The *main* point of the parable is found in the second half of the story, but the first half of the story is so powerful that we often focus on it and not the main point. (That's okay—the first half makes a great point, too!)

The image of the younger son asking for his share of the inheritance, running off and spending it, ending up in the pigsty, and then returning home only to have his father run out, throw his arms around him, put a ring on his finger and a robe on his back—it's a beautiful picture. But, remember the *context* of the parable—the Pharisees are grumbling about Jesus hanging out with sinners.

What does Jesus say heaven does when sinners repent?

The angels rejoice! So, the *main* point, not the *only* point, but the *main* point is in the second half of the parable, when the older son refuses to rejoice with the father over the younger son's repentance. That's the *main* point. Are we able to rejoice over God's love for sinners?

In verse 30, the older brother says to the father, "But when this son of yours came, who has devoured your property with prostitutes, you killed the fattened calf for him!"[3] The older son calls his brother "this son of yours."

He refuses to call him his brother.

The father responds, "Son, you are always with me, and all that is mine is yours. It was fitting to celebrate and be glad, for this your brother was dead, and is alive; he was lost, and is found."[4] The father affirms that the older son is his *son*, but then he reminds him that the younger son is his *brother*.

When I was younger, my favorite part of this parable was the father's running to the younger son and throwing his arms around him and lavishing him with grace. I couldn't fathom that kind of love.

But then I had children.

When I had children, the father's behavior made sense to me. There is *nowhere* my children could run where I wouldn't chase them. There is *nothing* they could do that I wouldn't forgive.

3. Luke 15:30.

4. Luke 15:31–32.

So, the story has changed for me to a convicting story—my focus has shifted to the older brother and the challenge set before him by the father. That was what I tried to convey in *my* story. I understand a father's love for his children. Am I able to extend that love to others?

When I encounter someone who doesn't deserve God's grace—am I able to see them the way God sees them? Can I call them "brother" and not "this son of yours"?

We're all familiar with the younger son's crisis and the decision he faced about whether or not he should go home. But, the older son faced that *same* crisis and that *same* decision. He didn't wander as far away from home, but he stood in the field while his father celebrated his brother. His father said to him, come home and celebrate with me.

The older son had to make a choice: Would he celebrate with the father? Would he come home?

Both sons were lost. Both sons were pursued by the father. Both sons were called home.

In verse 31, the father says to the older son, "You are always with me, and all that is mine is yours."

The older son's mind was on all the things he didn't have—he didn't get an early inheritance, he didn't get a fattened calf or even a goat, he didn't get a party.

But the older son had something that the younger son didn't have—he had a relationship with his father.

The father says to him, "You're always with me."

The younger son got an inheritance. He got a goat—probably many goats when he was in the far country. He got parties and our imaginations can run wild with all the other things he got. But there was one thing he didn't have in the far country—a dad. Or at least, a *relationship* with his dad.

Those who have lost their dad, or never had a dad, or never had a good relationship with their dad—if they were given a choice between which son they'd rather be, the choice is easy. Would you rather have a million bucks or a father?

Some of you come to Jesus's table as a younger son. You are in the far country. Maybe you're even in the pigsty. You *cannot* outrun God's grace. Come home and celebrate.

Some of you come to the table as an older son. You've chosen the harder path: the road of faithfulness. You're not sure if the Father sees your hard work and your toil, and you're growing weary. He is always with you and all he has is *yours*. Come home and celebrate.

QUESTIONS FOR REFLECTION

1. Have you ever been lost (in the woods, shopping mall, crowded place, etc.)? What was that like?

2. What is your immediate reaction to Jesus's parable? Who do you identify with the most—the younger son, the older son, or the father?

3. Have you ever been in "the far country" like the younger son? What was that like? How did Jesus bring you back?

4. Have you ever been in "the field" like the older son? What does that feel like?

5. How do you think the story ended? Did the older son come home and celebrate?

6. How can we better remember to rejoice at the repentance of sinners?

Conclusion

Jesus's message was simple: "The time is fulfilled, and the kingdom of God is at hand; repent and believe in the gospel."[1] Jesus Christ died for sins and rose from the dead. The kingdom is at hand!

In this book, I have highlighted ten parables of Jesus. He told plenty more, but you'll have to find them for yourself in the Gospels! These are the ten things I hope you walk away with after reading the ten parables.

God likes you. He's throwing a party in your honor. The kingdom of God is like a rich man throwing a party for his only child who has him wrapped around her finger. Guess what—*you* are the guest of honor. Jesus not only loves you, but he likes you and would love to celebrate with you.

Small acts of kindness have a big impact. The kingdom of God is like a viral video (or a mustard seed). It starts small, but God makes it big. You don't have to change the world to work for the kingdom of God—start with loving your neighbor. Volunteer at a food bank. Sponsor a child. Welcome a new family to your neighborhood. God does big things with small acts of kindness.

God hears you and he cares. Never stop praying. The kingdom of God is like a woman who wore down an insurance company that refused to pay her claim. If an uncaring insurance company eventually pays out if you pester them long enough, how much more a God who hears you and cares? Never give up praying!

Grace is not fair. This is a good thing! The kingdom of God is like a venture capitalist who volunteered to fund a computer software project. When it succeeded, he paid the last hired by the company the same as the founders. God has been gracious to you. He will be gracious to others, to some even more than to you. Celebrate with them!

1. Mark 1:15.

145

We cannot love God and show contempt for others. An addict and a PTA mom both went to church to pray. The PTA mom thanked God for her numerous successes—that she was a self-made woman and not a loser like her husband. The addict wouldn't even look up to heaven. He was transfixed on the broken body of Jesus and prayed, "God have mercy on me, a sinner." I tell you a truth, the addict and not the PTA mom went home justified before God.

The poor are our brothers and sisters. In the kingdom of God, the poor are our brothers and sisters. Listen to them. Learn from them. Treat them with dignity. They are created in the image of God and theirs is the kingdom!

God is good. Evil is real. Someday it will all make sense. The kingdom of God is like a legendary salesman who seemed unprepared for his presentation. His partner lost sleep worrying that the legends were untrue, but when it was time to present, he delivered! Evil and suffering are real. But God is good and he has defeated them on the cross. One day, this will all make sense.

Jesus has the words of eternal life. Keep the faith. The kingdom of God is like four coworkers in a weight loss competition. Some quit early, some get distracted, some persevere. Don't be discouraged by persecution; don't be distracted by wealth. Keep the faith.

Even our enemies are our neighbors. The kingdom of God is like a young woman who found herself in trouble. When the religious experts did not take the time to help her, compassion came from an unlikely place. Even our enemies are our neighbors. Show love and compassion to everyone.

Come home and celebrate. The kingdom of God is like a man with two sons. When one repented and came home, the other refused to call him brother. There is nowhere we can run where God will not chase us. There is nothing we can do he won't forgive. Come home and celebrate.

CPSIA information can be obtained
at www.ICGtesting.com
Printed in the USA
JSHW020551170323
39064JS00003B/9